P9-DXN-280

DISCARD

Library of Shakespearean Biography and Criticism

I. PRIMARY REFERENCE WORKS ON SHAKESPEARE

II. CRITICISM AND INTERPRETATION

   A. Textual Treatises, Commentaries
   B. Treatment of Special Subjects
   C. Dramatic and Literary Art in Shakespeare

III. SHAKESPEARE AND HIS TIME

   A. General Treatises. Biography
   B. The Age of Shakespeare
   C. Authorship

Series III, Part C

SHAKESPEARE'S MAGIC CIRCLE

𝔏ibrary of 𝔖hakespearean 𝔅iography and 𝔒riticism

SHAKESPEARE'S
MAGIC CIRCLE

by

ALFRED J. EVANS

BOOKS FOR LIBRARIES PRESS
FREEPORT, NEW YORK

First Published 1956

Reprinted 1970 by arrangement with Sir Martin J. Evans
and the literary agents, Collins-Knowlton-Wing, Inc.

INTERNATIONAL STANDARD BOOK NUMBER:

0-8369-5504-8

LIBRARY OF CONGRESS CATALOG CARD NUMBER:

72-128884

PRINTED IN THE UNITED STATES OF AMERICA

CONTENTS

PREFACE

THIS book was originally written before Dr. A. W. Titherley's remarkable and erudite work, *Shakespeare's Identity*, was published in March 1952, though it has been revised since then.

Dr. Titherley has been kind enough to read the draft and to make many valuable suggestions and corrections, for which I am deeply grateful; pointing out at the same time where he disagrees with me. The matters of disagreement between us concern some of the sonnets and are not of fundamental importance to the issues discussed here. With a few minor exceptions I have retained my own opinions.

Dr. Titherley is in no way responsible for my views or hypotheses or for the accuracy of any of the facts stated in the book, and it is only fair to say that he disagrees with the importance I attach to the "magic circle." In the appendices I have made considerable use of his researches and gratefully acknowledge my indebtedness.

The delay in publication has had the fortunate result of enabling me to include some very recent researches of Professor George Lambin, which are of outstanding importance.

Following Sir George Greenwood, I have used without prejudice and purely as a matter of convenience, the spelling "Shakespeare" when speaking of the author of the plays and poems, whoever he may be, and "Shakspere" when referring to William Shakspere of Stratford.

I have also employed the word "Stratfordian" when referring to those who believe that "Shakespeare" and "Shakspere" are identical.

INTRODUCTION

THE question of the authorship of the works of Shakespeare is by far the most interesting literary puzzle that has ever intrigued the world. Few of the general public realise the enormous strength of the case against Shakspere of Stratford and it is very tempting, in any new contribution to the vexed authorship controversy, to collect a mass of detail from numerous books and restate in three or four solid chapters the anti-Stratfordian argument. On the advice of my publishers I have refrained from doing this (with some regrets), and must refer those readers wishing to become conversant with the case against William of Stratford to some of the books where it has already been brilliantly set out. Most of these books have been written to advocate the claims of some other candidate. Mr. J. Thomas Looney, for instance, tries to demonstrate in *Shakespeare Identified* (1919) that the 17th Earl of Oxford was the real Shakespeare, and devotes most of his first eighty-nine pages to an admirable anti-Stratfordian essay. Mr. Ignatius Donnelly, in *The Great Cryptogram,* wrote a highly unconvincing book in favour of candidature of Francis Bacon, though the first hundred pages contain a mass of evidence against the Stratford actor as the author, which in general has never been refuted. Sir George Greenwood, almost alone, made no claim to know who wrote the works of Shakespeare. He called himself an " agnostic " and in a scholarly but eminently readable book, *The Shakespeare Problem Restated* (1916), made out the most convincing anti-Stratfordian case that has yet been produced. Lastly, for those who wish to dig even deeper, there is Dr. A. W. Titherley's great work, *Shakespeare's Identity* (1952), advocating the claims of the 6th Earl of Derby and adding a staggering mass of new evidence relating to the general problem.   There are many other books on this subject, but the above are sufficient to enable any interested reader to obtain ample information.   The following is a very brief sketch of the fundamental reasons for discarding William Shakspere of Stratford.

[1] William's father, mother and his daughter Judith were all illiterate in the sense that they used a " mark " instead of signing their names.[2]   William was baptised on April 26th, 1564. Nothing whatever is known of his childhood.   It is presumed that he went to school at the Stratford Free School, and tradition, which may or may not be true, says that he attended the school from the age of eight to the age of thirteen, after which, till he left home (probably in 1587), he was in his father's trade of glover and butcher.

In 1582, according to a marriage bond, when about to marry Anne Whateley, he appears to have been compelled to marry Anne Hathaway, who was eight years his senior.   Their first child was baptised about six months after the marriage.   The twins, Hamnet and Judith, arrived in 1585 and nothing more is known of his life at Stratford then.   The next reliable information about him is that in 1594 he appears as a member of the famous Lord Chamberlain's company, which till April of that year had been under the patronage of Lord Strange, the eldest son of the 4th Earl of Derby.   But by the end of 1594 twelve Shakespeare plays, two long poems and many sonnets had been written, and among the earliest plays are four with pure French or Italian backgrounds.   *Love's Labour's Lost*, for instance, portrays many historically accurate episodes at the court of Henri of Navarre at Nerac, in the South of France, between 1578 and 1583.   The principal characters are easily recognisable French aristocrats whose individualities are in no doubt.   *Two Gentlemen of Verona,*

[1] Reprinted by permission from *The Courier*, January 1955.
[2] See A. R. W. Anders *Shakespeare's Books*, page 10, note 2.   Also Halliwell-Phillipps who says, " Although both Shakespeare's parents were absolutely illiterate ".

also one of the earliest plays, shows that Shakespeare had a most intimate topographical knowledge of Milan and the intricate waterways of Northern Italy. *The Merchant of Venice* not only exudes a pure Italian atmosphere but shows real knowledge of the laws of Venice and the complicated Italian politics of the day. It is impossible to believe that *Romeo and Juliet* and *The Taming of the Shrew* could have been written by someone who had never visited Verona and Padua or did not know at first hand the customs and habits of the Italians. *The Comedy of Errors*, another early play, was founded on the *Menaechmi* of Plautus, of which there was no translation at the time ; and there is much additional evidence that Shakespeare could read French, Latin and Italian authors in the originals. Moreover there are no signs of a Warwickshire patois in any of the plays. Surely an astonishing fact.

The early historical plays are partly set in France, and an incredible amount of reading would have been necessary before a young man with Shakspere's scanty education could even conceive such plays. Genius can account for much, but it cannot supply the multitudinous facts of special experience which Shakespeare reveals even in his earliest plays. Nor can it account for such a profound knowledge of the English language, greater than any other man has ever possessed.[1]

But this is not the whole marvel—for young Shakspere, if indeed he wrote the plays, besides absorbing a mass of information on Italy, France, Latin, law, history and English would have had many other things to learn. The astonishing thing is that every expert, whether he be a lawyer, scholar, linguist, traveller, soldier, hunter, herald, courtier, seaman, magician, actor, fencer, philosopher, horseman, philologist, humanitarian, lover or poet, is convinced that Shakespeare was also an expert

[1] In his book, *The Shakespeare Symphony* (1906), Harold Bayley estimated that Shakespeare introduced 9450 new words into the English language, Sir Thomas Browne 2850, Francis Bacon 1850, George Chapman 1500, Ben Jonson 1350.

in his own department of knowledge. In 1593 Shakespeare published a *de luxe* edition of *Venus and Adonis*, perhaps the most cultured and polished epic in the English language, displaying much learning and a deep knowledge of Ovid and classical Greek mythology. He dedicated it to the young Earl of Southampton in terms of such easy familiarity, unlike the usual sycophantic dedications of the period, as to imply personal friendship.

In 1594 he dedicated the poem *Lucrece*, also to Southampton, in terms of even closer friendship such as one peer might use to another. The status of actors in those days being extremely low, it is fantastically improbable that in 1593 the Stratford "rustic" could be an intimate friend of the great Earl of Southampton. Indeed, prolonged and careful research has in fact never discovered any connection at all between Southampton and William Shakspere of Stratford. Ben Jonson, who appears to have disliked the actor, mocked him in a play as an ignorant rustic and in 1616 published a scornful epigram accusing him of plagiarism—the very year of Shakspere's death. No letter that Shakspere wrote exists and only two mention his name ; both being concerned solely with money-lending. When Shakspere returned to Stratford about the turn of the century, he became a land-owner and money-lender for the rest of his life ; yet during this period the great plays continued to pour out. Though Shakspere's name spelt in numerous ways is mentioned in lists of actors and in legal documents, no indication is ever given that distinguishes him from his fellow actors. When he died no poet wrote an ode to his memory as was done when Spenser, Jonson and other even minor poets died. Nor is there any mention of books or plays or manuscripts in his will which otherwise makes a most careful distribution of his possessions. Finally, the evidence that this uncultured actor wrote the stupendous works of Shakespeare has been shown to be of the flimsiest kind.

CHAPTER I

SHAKESPEARE, BACON, RUTLAND AND DERBY

IN all the history of literature there is no instance in which the personal character of a prolific author of fiction is not in some way, and often very clearly, reflected in his works. Yet it is the orthodox Stratfordian dogma that Shakspere wrote his plays objectively—that is to say, they were only in the dimmest way, if at all, a reflection of his own first-hand experiences in life. Shakspere had, say the pundits, no great crisis in his life which caused the Great Tragedies to pour from his mind and pen. He experienced no passionate love, which, being unrequited, tore his soul to pieces. The sonnets were rather exercises in poetic composition than cries from a wounded heart. Shakspere it seems gained the remarkable mass of knowledge, which is undoubtedly in the plays, merely second hand, by reading or by conversation. It is therefore useless, we are told, to investigate Shakspere's life in order to obtain a better understanding of the plays ; and we are asked to believe all this !

Let us, therefore, from an examination of the plays, see what kind of man we should in reason expect to have written the great works.

(1) First, there is no avoiding the conclusion that Shakespeare was an aristocrat—it is self evident. Even *The Merry Wives of Windsor*, one of the two plays which deals with middle-class life, drags in the Garter ceremonies and The Star Chamber. Kings, queens, dukes and Court life are clearly the *milieu* in which Shakespeare is happiest. Even when the scene is rural, as in *As You Like It*, the Court moves into the country. The point of view is manifestly that of a nobleman looking on peasant life

13

from above. There is an air of feudalism in almost every play. The retainers and servants of the noble characters are marvellously drawn, but Shakespeare shows very little familiarity with village life and the plays are exactly what might have been expected from a courtier and a scholar. If a man from the lower classes wrote them, it is amazing that he has avoided introducing scenes from his own humble environment and still more amazing that he could have acquired such intimate knowledge of a mode of life so far above his own.

The education of Shakespeare as revealed by his works is what every nobleman in the times of Elizabeth had an opportunity of obtaining. Whilst a boy every aristocrat had a private tutor : when twelve to fifteen years of age he usually went to Oxford or Cambridge and afterwards to the Inns of Court to study Law. His education would be " finished " by several months or years abroad. One can only add that Shakespeare seems to have made the very fullest use of such opportunities.

(2) Shakespeare had strong Lancastrian leanings. The Henry VI trilogy, *Richard II* and *Richard III* are sufficient proof of this.

(3) He was a passionate lover of music, knowing full well its magic power in drama, e.g., *The Merchant of Venice*, *Twelfth Night* and the many songs scattered throughout the plays.

(4) He was a skilled judge of a horse with great knowledge of hunting—more particularly of falconry, that form which was exclusively the sport of the aristocracy, but he also had humanitarian instincts : pity for the hunted hare (*Venus and Adonis*) and for the wounded deer (*As You Like It*), unusual in that age.

(5) He was a man without very strong religious convictions, but seems more familiar with Catholicism and the ways of Catholic priests than with Protestantism. He was certainly not a Puritan (*Romeo and Juliet*, *Hamlet*, etc.).

(6) He had deep interest in Magic, Astronomy, Astrology, Alchemy, Philosophy and Heraldry.

(7) He had travelled abroad very extensively, being specially familiar with the towns of Northern Italy. He understood French, Italian and Latin (*Henry V, Merchant of Venice, Othello, Comedy of Errors* and *Love's Labour's Lost*, etc.).

(8) He had unusually intimate experience of ships and storms at sea (*Twelfth Night, The Tempest, Pericles*).

(9) He loved flowers and knew a lot about forestry, but his observations on natural history sometimes reflected current errors (*The Winter's Tale, As You Like It*).

(10) He had wide technical knowledge of Law, which suggests that he passed through the Law schools at one or more of the Inns of Court. Shakespeare seems to take keen pleasure in exhibiting his legal versatility (*Henry IV, part 2, Measure For Measure*, etc.).

(11) His attitude towards women is conflicting. On the one hand we have the very young innocent, passionate and tragic girls, like Ophelia, Juliet, Desdemona and Imogen. On the other hand many of his women are highly intelligent, sophisticated and rather sex-conscious, such as Portia, Nerissa, Viola, Rosalind and Julia. Shakespeare obviously enjoys dressing them up in boy's clothes.

(12) He is careless about money matters and despises gold with such bitterness that we may believe he had suffered acutely from financial troubles.

> *Henry IV* . . . How quickly nature falls into revolt,
>   When gold becomes her object!
> *Romeo and Juliet* . . . There is thy gold, worse poison to men's souls.
> *Merchant of Venice* . . . Execration of Usury.
> *Timon of Athens* . . . Money is the root of evil.

(13) Shakespeare was of course an ardent dramatic enthusiast, but obviously also an actor, though not necessarily a professional actor and it would be most natural to suppose him to be a great lord, like Hamlet, who patronised a troupe of actors (*Hamlet*).

(14) He must have had a well-stocked library with leisure to study and write. Between the years 1590 and 1613 he was so fully occupied in writing and revising plays, that, if he was a nobleman, he could not have taken much part in affairs of state. We should expect Shakespeare to be a man who had largely withdrawn from politics, of whom history during those years would therefore have little to tell us.

(15) His object in writing the plays was most certainly not to make money but arose from sheer love of art and the insistent urge of a creative instinct.[1]

(16) He had probably fought a duel (*Romeo and Juliet, Hamlet, Twelfth Night*).

(17) His description of the siege of Harfleur in *Henry V* is so detailed and vivid that Shakespeare must have had personal experience of a siege. He certainly had first-hand knowledge of war.

(18) He had an astounding command of the English language, and used 15,000 different words—some say 20,000—when 8,000 sufficed for Milton.

With this broad specification of the poet, as inferred solely from the plays, no one in reason, orthodox or heretic, can fail to agree. In detail it may be questioned, but in general it is indubitably correct. The facts are in the plays plain for everyone who is not prejudiced to see.

We are asked to believe that an ill-educated actor by his supposed genius, his retentive memory, his wit, his charm and his prodigious industry (for which there is no evidence), was enabled to write masterpieces in the manner of a man with the foregoing versatile qualifications, experiences and education. But the truth is that the Stratfordians have never been able to demonstrate that the actor had any qualifications in the least approaching these. There is no record of his conversation ; no book with his signature in it has ever been found ; no one has

---

[1] See pages 44–5.

preserved a letter from him nor has any connection ever been traced, in spite of centuries of scholarly effort, between the actor and any of the aristocracy.

But Shakspere wrote the works of Shakespeare—Jonson said so—so runs the thin thread of argument. The dedication to *Venus and Lucrece* proves (by begging the question) that Shakspere was an intimate friend of Southampton ; and, if you only have faith in his genius all the rest follows. There is no need for further explanations say the Stratfordians. But there are increasing numbers of lovers of Shakespeare, who are far from satisfied with all this. Perhaps the clearest testimony against the actor is Shakespeare's enormous vocabulary, when we consider that even a University-trained Englishman, in these days of unlimited books, seldom commands more than 4,000 words.

But if Shakspere of Stratford did not write the plays who did ?

The plausible candidates who have been put forward all conform more or less closely to my summarised specification and obviously it would be futile to go into the highways and byways for a non-aristocratic candidate who would immediately be involved in many inconsistencies similar to those which make Shakspere of Stratford's candidature so impossible of acceptance. Impressive claims have been made severally for Francis Bacon, the Earls of Rutland, Derby and Oxford. Let us then consider each of them shortly.

Francis Bacon. Without any question there are between the prose works of Bacon and the works of Shakespeare many parallelisms. Either Bacon was Shakespeare or whoever was Shakespeare had access to the vast mass of knowledge possessed by Bacon. That the wisdom of Bacon contributed in packing some of the plays with learning and philosophy I personally have no doubt whatever. This I think the Baconians have fully proved. Unfortunately some Baconians have greatly overstated their case, and by putting far too much significance on ciphers and parallelisms have even tried to show that Bacon wrote most of the best literature of that age ! All that has emerged is that mere parallelisms are not dependable as evidence of identical authorship. Plagiarism was frequent in the literary world of those days and Shakespeare though not a plagiarist was a prince of borrowers. When he came across something which seemed to him good or interesting, whether scientific, philosophic, literary or legal, he had no hesitation in bringing it into his plays—often dragging it in. But that kind of borrowing requires many books, the right personal contacts and above all ample time for study.

What then are the grounds for refusing to believe that Bacon wrote the plays ? Bacon, in my opinion, has eliminated himself from the contest by his own pen. As a writer of prose he is superb, as a poet he is decidedly inferior—quite definitely below the Shakespearean standard. The same pen, which wrote Bacon's works and especially the essays, could not have written the plays of Shakespeare. The style and the whole attitude of mind are entirely different. Bacon simply had not in him that sympathetic understanding of passionate love which would have enabled him to compose *Romeo and Juliet* and *Othello* still less the fantastic mind to write *Love's Labour's Lost*, or *Midsummer Night's Dream*, and to create Falstaff.

Then there is the question of output. Bacon's *Life and Works*, edited by Spedding and Ellis, occupy fourteen 8vo volumes, but a great deal of this space is taken by prefaces, notes and comments, etc. In the opinion of Mr. Theobald,[1] whose purpose is to show how small Bacon's output really was, the total writings of Bacon could be contained in six such volumes each containing 520 pages. This is not a great output for a popular novelist, but it is a very large output considering the nature and contents of these books. If, on top of this, we place the whole works

---

[1] *Shakespeare in a Baconian Light*, by R. M. Theobald.

of Shakespeare, including the continual revision of the plays, we are going far beyond the capacity of any man—even Bacon.

Nor is it possible to believe that Bacon's tidy mind would have permitted his (supposed) dramatic works to have been scattered round, hacked about, mutilated and in fact left at the mercy of any half-educated theatre-scribe who chose to maltreat them. Would Bacon have permitted his precious plays, of which the author certainly knew the full value, to be issued in the First Folio with such an indescribable mess of blunders, printer's errors and garbled sentences? It is unbelievable. Did Bacon keep no fair copies of his works? If so what happened to them? For no man has ever been more conscious of posterity or desired its praise than Bacon. It is possible to imagine a cause for secrecy as to his authorship during his lifetime, but it is quite impossible to believe that such a man would have been content to rely on the alleged cryptograms and biliteral cyphers to ensure himself everlasting fame as a poet.

Whole libraries-full have been written on the Shakespeare-Bacon controversy, and I do not imagine for a moment that the few words I have written here will shake the faith of one single Baconian. On this question most people have immutably made up their minds—as I have.

Roger Manners, 5th Earl of Rutland. Both M. Demblon [1] in France and Mr. Sykes [2] have made out interesting claims for Rutland as Shakespeare. Being a scholar, a linguist, a traveller and an aristocrat he conforms in several respects with my specification for Shakespeare. He had a well-filled library at Belvoir in which were to be found many of the books utilised by Shakespeare. Rutland went up to Cambridge in 1590, and in 1596 visited Paris as well as those Italian towns which form the background of several of Shakespeare's plays. He was admitted

---

[1] M. Demblon's *Lord Rutland est Shakespeare.*
[2] *Alias William Shakespeare,* by C. W. Sykes.

to Gray's Inn in 1598. He went on an expedition to the Azores (*The Tempest*) and to Ireland with the Earl of Essex in 1599—which enabled him, so say his supporters, to write *Henry V*. Mr. Sykes lays great stress on the fact that Rutland had a brother with whom he was on bad terms and there are several instances of troublesome brothers in the plays. Also there are in the plays a number of words which are said to be exclusively Cambridge slang. Both these points as evidence of authorship seem to me to carry very little weight.

Rutland died June 26th, 1612, having, says Mr. Sykes, first written *The Tempest* to say farewell for ever, though the tenor of the play suggests that it was written by a man about to retire, not about to die.

Was Rutland Shakespeare? I am quite confident that he was not.

In the first place no rumour or hint has come down to us that Rutland was a poet or dramatist. Not even Mr. Sykes has been able to find a single allusion which refers (or could be twisted into referring) to Rutland as Shakespeare. Secondly, Rutland was born on October 6th, 1576, so that he was too young to be Shakespeare, for *Venus and Adonis* was published on April 18th, 1593, when Rutland was sixteen years and six months old. Let us suppose that it was written during the previous year, though it was probably written many years earlier. Is it conceivable that a poem of such mature scholarship could be the work of a boy of only just sixteen or less? It is equally difficult, if not more so, to believe that *Lucrece* was composed by a boy of barely seventeen.

The dates on which some of Shakespeare's plays were written are very uncertain.[1] The latest dates given by Sir Edmund Chambers are on the average considerably later than those given by earlier scholars. This redating, which is really essential

---

[1] Though Dr. Titherley, by his new method, has now dated the plays with far greater certainty than hitherto.

to the case for Shakspere of Stratford, is also of great advantage to the case for Rutland. Even so, taking Chambers's dates for the composition of the plays, we get no less than nine plays written before the end of 1594. Had Rutland been Shakespeare, then (according to Chambers) he wrote *Henry VI*, parts *I*, *II*, *III*, *Richard III*, *Comedy of Errors*, *Titus Andronicus*, *Love's Labour's Lost*, *Romeo and Juliet*, *The Taming of the Shrew*, and in addition, *Venus and Adonis*, *Lucrece* and most of the sonnets before he was seventeen years old. It is unbelievable. In any case Rutland did not visit Italy till 1596 so that the composition of many of the earlier Italian-based plays has to be postponed till after that date—a proposition which, on critical evidence, is entirely unacceptable.

Finally, the Sonnets. Here the upper date limit, at any rate for the majority, is 1598, when Shakespeare's sonnets are mentioned by Meres. 1591 to 1595 are the reasonably certain dates between which most of the Sonnets were written ; that is to say when Rutland was from fifteen to nineteen years old. Now it is obvious that many of the Sonnets show a profound knowledge of the world and were addressed by an older man of experience to a youth ; certainly not by a boy to another boy, e.g., the Earl of Southampton, three years Rutland's senior.

The 6th Earl of Derby. In 1560 or 1561, a second son was born in London to Margaret Clifford, the wife of Henry Lord Strange who later became the 4th Earl of Derby. The child was known as William Stanley and his elder brother, Ferdinando, who became the 5th Earl in 1593, was two years older than William. The two boys were brought up as pages in the Court and were thoroughly familiar with Court life. Owing to the marriage of Henry Lord Strange with a great granddaughter of Henry VII, (Margaret Clifford) his two sons, Ferdinando and William, were sufficiently close to the throne to be candidates for the succession to Queen Elizabeth, and indeed the only legal ones by the Act of Succession of 1544.

In fact, both William and Ferdinando were considered by the Roman Catholics to be the proper claimants to the throne, but for various reasons, one being that Ferdinando had married beneath him (the daughter of a mere knight, Sir John Spencer), William was preferred by Father Parsons above all others (p. 97).

In 1593, just after he had become the 5th Earl of Derby, Ferdinando was approached by the Catholics, but refusing to act in any way traitorously to Elizabeth he actually delivered over to justice the Jesuit agent, Richard Hesketh, who was acting on behalf of the subversive Catholic party abroad. Hesketh was promptly executed, and it seems likely that Ferdinando, who died a mysterious death a few months later, was poisoned by the Jesuits in revenge.

Probably much of the early days of the two boys was spent at Meriden Manor in North Warwickshire, which is reputed to be the very centre of England and was one of the pleasantest of the Derby seats. It is in the old forest of Arden near Polesworth, where Holinshed, the historian, from whom so much of Shakespeare's history is taken, lived and where he died in 1580.

All round Polesworth and on the route between North Warwickshire and London are various places which Shakespeare mentions in his plays—Tamworth, Sutton Coldfield, Hinckley, Greet (Greece), Barston, Coventry, Kenilworth, Rugby, Warwick, Southam, Dunsmore Heath and Daventry. There is even a Wincot a mile or two from Polesworth, which is far more likely to be the scene of Sly's tippling than the Wilmecot or Wincot near Stratford. The Wincot near Stratford was described by Atkyns in 1712 as consisting only of two houses. "It is extremely unlikely that here was to be found an alehouse of any kind," says Mr. Halliwell-Phillipps, while the Wincot ale of North Warwickshire was renowned. William Stanley, even as a boy, and certainly as a man, was thoroughly familiar with the road between North Warwickshire and London. This is

Staffordshire

Leicestershire

Tamworth

Polesworth

Wincote

Sutton Coldfield

Hinckley

Birmingham

Greet?

Forest of Arden Woodland

Coventry

River Avon

Meriden

Barston

Kenilworth?

Rugby

Dunsmore Heath

Warwick

Worcestershire

Stratford on Avon

Feldon

Southam

Daventry

Northampton -shire

River Avon

Gloucestershire

Cotswold Hills

Barton on the Heath

Oxfordshire

The County of Warwickshire
Places underlined are mentioned in the plays.

the route to London that Shakespeare knew so well,[1] but there is no evidence in the plays that he knew the route from Stratford to London.

The Earls of Derby had for a century or more been intensely interested in the drama. Even the first Lord Derby, who is conspicuous in *Richard III* as Lord Thomas Stanley, took part in the *Mystery of the Assumption*, a religious play, at High Cross, Chester. The 4th Earl, William's father, was a man of highest culture, and *persona grata* with the French Court. He was also a somewhat straight-laced Protestant, but this did not prevent him having a number of natural children, of whom one was Ursula, who married Sir John Salisbury.[2]

Young William was in fact from his earliest days brought up in the midst of dramatic activity, and amateur theatricals were no doubt one of the main amusements of the family. When eleven years old William Stanley went up to St. John's College, Oxford, which was noted in those days for its cultivation of drama. From Oxford he went to the Law Schools in London, where he was enrolled first at Gray's Inn and then at Lincoln Inn. When about twenty-one years old, in 1582, William Stanley obtained leave to travel abroad with his tutor Richard Lloyd, and the two of them arrived in Paris on July 27th. We know from two letters preserved among Elizabeth's State papers that William, because of his parentage, was well received at the Court of Henri III, for his father, the 4th Earl, after being at this court in 1550 as a hostage, was greatly welcomed when he returned in 1585 to present Henri III with the insignia of the Order of the Garter.

To have a working knowledge of Latin and to be able to speak French fluently were among the normal accomplishments of the Elizabethan aristocracy. William had the reputation of being an unusually studious and intelligent youth, so that we

[1] See Falstaff's march for instance. *Outlines II*, page 307.
[2] See *Love's Martyr*, Allusion 16, Ch. VI.

can be sure from the first the language presented no difficulties.[1]
From Paris, Stanley and his tutor, Lloyd, travelled to Blois,
Tour, Orleans, Saumur and Angers. In a letter to Walsingham,
Lloyd acknowledges the receipt of Stanley's licence to travel
and informs Walsingham that he intends to establish his pupil
in the neighbourhood of Angers for the winter, if he can discover
a suitable " retreat " away from the main road.

This letter is dated October 6th, 1582, and one wonders what
could have been the purpose of this retirement from the Parisian
world.[2]

A little book, printed by Nuttall, entitled *A brief account of the
travels of the celebrated Sir William Stanley, son of the 4th Earl of
Derby of Lathom House, Lancashire*, gives us an account of
Stanley's extensive travels, some of them obviously legendary,
but from this account we know that after leaving France, Stanley
visited Spain, where he fought a duel or duels and escaped
disguised as a Friar. This adventure is supposed to have taken
place in 1583, and on his way to Spain, Stanley could not have
failed to visit the then-famous Court of Navarre, though
documentary evidence is lacking.

There is however a letter, dated June 9th, 1583, from Cobham
to Walsingham, from which we learn that the King of Navarre
was " in good health at Bearn having furnished his Court with
principal gentlemen of religion (Protestant) and reformed his
house." Cobham goes on to say that many nobles and Protest-
ants and Papists had arrived at the Court of Navarre, also that
many persons of quality intended to visit it and others had sent
their children, recognising the honourable order which existed

---

[1] See *Ancient and Honourable House of Stanley* (Seacome, 1741).
[2] Is it possible that Stanley had already decided to work on the draft of *The Troublesome
Raigne of King Jhon*, inspired by the walls and plains of Angers ?
   Shakespeare's play *King John* is certainly one of his early productions. In the *Troublesome Raigne* there are powerful glimpses of Shakespeare's mind and certainly Shakespeare
made such free use of it in writing *King John* that the author of the former play might
have complained if the same pen had not written both. Or, alternatively, did Stanley
retire to Angers for the purpose of making a first draft of *Measure for Measure* ? (see p. 116).

there.   This is approximately the date at which we may be sure
that Stanley and his tutor, Richard Lloyd, visited the Court of
Navarre at Nerac.

Monsieur Montégut, well known in France as a translator of
Shakespeare and a literary critic of the highest reputation,
speaking of the play *Love's Labour's Lost*, writes as follows :

(Translated) " It is extraordinary to see how Shakespeare is
faithful down to the most minute details to the true history and
to the local colour.   Just as all the details in *Romeo and Juliet,
The Merchant of Venice* and *Othello* are Italian, so all the details
of this piece (*Love's Labour's Lost*) are French.   The style of
conversation of the men and women is completely French,
lively, alert and witty ;   an endless game of battledore and
shuttlecock, a skirmish of wit, a little war of repartees.   Even
the errors in taste are totally French, and the language is
sharpened and over-refined to a point of witty preciousness,
which has never displeased the French, particularly the upper
classes."

Monsieur Montégut goes on to note that the way the
characters hide their affections under a mask of gaiety and their
passions under a veil of mockery is particularly French—so also
is their fear of ridicule.   And all this is conveyed, he says, not
only with the delicacy and competence of a master mind which
thoroughly understood the virtues and weaknesses of the French
character, but of a mind which was essentially aristocratic.

Professor Abel Lefranc[1] has clearly demonstrated that the
author of *Love's Labour's Lost* must himself have witnessed the
main incidents of the play taking place before his eyes at the
Court of Navarre and have heard recounted to him on the spot,
by those who had participated, the story of the actual Oath of
Austerity sworn by Henri of Navarre and his courtiers.

The play follows the historical facts with astonishing fidelity ;
indeed the main characters can be readily identified with men

---

[1] *Sous le Masque de William Shakespeare*, by Abel Lefranc.

and women of the French noblesse who are known to have been at the Court of Navarre at that time. Thus the King, though he is called Ferdinand, possibly after William's elder brother, is certainly Henri of Navarre, the evergreen lover whose peculiarities in writing in the margin of his love letters or spurring his horse violently, etc., are all reproduced faithfully in the play.

Biron is Charles de Goncourt, Baron de Biron, a great friend of the King and also of William Stanley, at least when he was the Earl of Derby, for Derby met him at Gravesend when Biron later visited England. Longueville is the Duc de Longeville. Dumaine is probably the Duc de Mayenne, who may have been friendly with the King at that time, but was later his enemy. Boyet (Guy de Pibrac) and Mercade were courtiers, and La Motte was an equerry at the Court of Navarre, and Armado, the fantastical Spaniard, may have come to life from a memory of some Spaniard whom Stanley had met during his adventurous voyage in Spain. As for the Princess of France, there cannot be a doubt that she is a perfect portrait of Marguerite de Valois, daughter of Catherine de Medici and the estranged wife of the King of Navarre.

Marguerite and her mother had arrived at Nerac in 1578 for the purpose of recapturing the heart of her husband and discussing the important topic of her dowry which included Aquitaine. Diplomacy was supported by a bevy of lovely ladies-in-waiting, who for their grace and flightiness were known as *l'escadron volant*. The negotiations were conducted, as Professor Lefranc pointed out, in an atmosphere of gallantry, pageantry and continual entertainment which is strikingly similar to that which we find in the play. Sully wrote of the occasion : *On se livra au plaisir, aux festins et aux fêtes galantes, ne nous amusant tous qu' à rire, danser et courir la bague.*

Just before this visit Marguerite had made journeys exactly corresponding to those referred to by the Princess and her ladies in Act II, Scene I of the play : to Alençon (Marguerite's brother Francois was Duke of Alençon) in 1578 and to Liège Brabant in 1577. ("Did I not dance with you in Brabant," says Biron to Rosaline.) It was at Liège that Helen de Tournon,[1] daughter of Queen Marguerite's principal lady-in-waiting, died of love for a young nobleman, the Marquis of Varambon. The Marquis was not in Liège at the time of her death and only learnt of it when, returning, he met the funeral procession. It seems certain that this incident is reflected not only in the death of Katharine's sister (Act V) but in the story of the death and burial of Ophelia in *Hamlet* (Act V), and it was not made known till years later when Marguerite's Memoirs were published in 1628.

We know, in fact, beyond all question that the background of *Love's Labour's Lost* reveals accurate and intimate knowledge of the Court of Navarre and it can hardly be doubted that the picture is drawn by an actual eyewitness.

The absurd interlude, "The Nine Worthies," which is intro-into *Love's Labour's Lost*, also proves that the author of the play was closely acquainted with William Stanley's tutor, Richard Lloyd, at about this time (1582–3). Richard Lloyd [2] was a true pedant, being in fact the author of a pompous "discourse" or pageant called *The Nine Worthies*, which is unquestionably the original of that parodied by Shakespeare with such mild satire and humour. *The Nine Worthies*, by Lloyd, was printed "by R. Warde at the Sign of the Talbot, neere Holborne Circuit in 1584." Lloyd appears to have returned to England after the visit to Navarre, for we do not hear of him during the last years of Stanley's voyages abroad. Perhaps Stanley had had more than enough of his tiresome and pedantic tutor. But it cannot

---

[1] According to Professor Lambin she was also the original of Helena in *All's Well that Ends Well*, p. 113.

[2] Lloyd was born at Shrewsbury in 1545. He went to France in 1580 as protégé of the Earl of Leicester. He knew John Dee the astrologer, who was a friend of the Derby family. He wrote a letter to James I interlarded with Latin.

be doubted that he is the original of Holofernes,[1] for the coincidences throughout are too remarkable to avoid this conclusion. Many years later, we may note, Richard Lloyd's *Nine Worthies* was " given " at Chester, Derby's home town.

Perhaps, at Angers, whilst William Stanley was drafting *The Troublesome Raigne of King John,* Lloyd was composing *The Nine Worthies.* We may even ask whether Lloyd insisted on putting on his pedantic play before the Court of Navarre ? It almost seems so.

Orthodoxy now accepts the above source of the play and some Stratfordians may suggest that when Stanley returned home he gave to Shakspere all the details of his experiences at the Court of Navarre so that the actor could then write *Love's Labour's Lost* ! That William Stanley after his return to England should have met Shakspere, the actor, is most probable, for the Lord Chamberlain's company, in which we find Shakspere in 1594, had been for some years previously under the patronage of Stanley's brother, Lord Strange. But the very brilliance of *Love's Labour's Lost* makes it the most impossible play, with its quips and quirks and flights of fancy, intimate touches and accurate local colour, to have been written second-hand even by a scholar from a description by another.

Nuttall's narrative describes how Stanley spent three years in Italy visiting monuments and places of interest. Other reports of his extended travels are often too mythical for much reliance in detail to be placed upon them, but Stanley certainly had a great reputation as a traveller—Poland, Egypt, Palestine, Turkey and Russia being among the places included in his recorded journeys. He had ample time and opportunity to become really familiar with the towns of Northern Italy which figure so repeatedly and realistically in the plays—Padua, Mantua, Verona, Milan and Venice and Florence.

---

[1] Gargantua's tutor (from Rabelais) was named Holoferne, which is a very suitable nickname for Lloyd, probably given to him by the courtiers of Nerac.

That Shakespeare had a very detailed knowledge of Northern Italy there can be no disputing and Italian scholars of today insist that the poet himself actually visited Italy ; a point of highest importance in this investigation, because Shakspere of Stratford never left England so far as is known.

We must consider it here.[1]

Sir Edward Sullivan, an orthodox Stratfordian, in articles he wrote for the 1918 January and February numbers of *The Nineteenth Century*, demonstrated, beyond reasonable doubt, that Shakespeare was extremely familiar with Northern Italy. He writes " that his (Shakespeare's) *knowledge of the Italian language,* coupled with what he may have gathered from hearsay, enabled him to describe with accuracy the waterways of the country and also to read in their original form some of the romances and dramatic writing on which the plots or the incidents of his plays were based."

So one Stratfordian at any rate considered that Shakespeare somehow acquired enough Italian to read an Italian play.[2]

Now when did Shakspere of Stratford have time and opportunity to learn Italian and acquire such detailed knowledge of the topography of Northern Italy, amongst all his other multifarious occupations ?

Dr. Karl Elze in his well-known Essays (1873) has no doubt whatever that Shakespeare visited Italy and, as noted, several Italian scholars concur.[3] It is indeed hard to believe that *The Merchant of Venice* could have been written by someone who did not know Venice and the Rialto from personal experience.

---

[1] Some of these examples are taken from *New Views for Old*, Roderick Eagle, 1930.

[2] Sir Edward also shows conclusively that Shakespeare was perfectly correct when in *The Two Gentlemen of Verona* he connects Verona and Milan by a waterway. See p. 122. For many years the Stratfordians have quoted this supposed error of Shakespeare's as a proof of his ignorance of the geography of Northern Italy. It seems now that Shakespeare was right and the Stratfordians were wrong.

[3] Notably Professor Grillo and Dr. Colafelice of Verona.

Here are a few instances illustrating Shakespeare's personal knowledge of Italy, and the reader should remember the very real difficulties which existed in those days in obtaining accurate information about foreign countries. Today one can go to a lending library and, with the help of travel books, a Baedeker for instance, one can discover minute details about any place in Europe with the greatest ease. But in Queen Elizabeth's time there were no lending libraries and very few books or maps. Shakespeare's intimacy with Italy, if he did not go there, would be staggering ; in truth nothing but a prolonged stay in Northern Italy can account for so much local knowledge.

(1) In *The Merchant of Venice* we find :

> Unto the tranect, to the common ferry
> Which trades to Venice.

At one time the meaning of " tranect " was a mystery, but it is certainly a misprint for tragect—that is to say *traghetti*, the anglicised word for a ferry in Venice. There was a common ferry at two places, Fasina and Merse, and obviously Shakespeare knew there was such a ferry.

(2) According to Mr. C. A. Brown's[1] *Studies in the History of Venice*, Dr. Bellario's namesakes live in Padua to this day.

Padua was of course the right place from which to fetch a " learned doctor," for the reputation of the University of Padua in those days was such that no degrees were recognised by the Venetian Senate but those of Padua.

(3) Shylock's confidence that he will receive justice is true to fact. Antonio recognises this when he says :

> The duke cannot deny the course of law
> For the commodity that strangers have
> With us in Venice, if it be denied,
> Will much impeach the justice of his state ;
> Since that the trade and profit of the city
> Consisteth of all nations.

---

[1] Also *Shakespeare's Autographical Poems*, by C. A. Brown.

Mr. Brown comments : " That states the truth about Venetian commercial policy ; the great freedom and security she always allowed to strangers accounted for much of her prosperity."

(4) Charles Knight, in reference to *The Taming of the Shrew*, said :

" It is difficult for those who have explored the city of Padua to resist the persuasion that the poet himself had been one of the travellers who had come from afar to look upon its seat of learning, if not to partake of its ' ingenious studies.' There is a pure Paduan atmosphere hanging about this play."

(5) The names of the characters in the plays are chosen with an accurate knowledge of Italian customs and people. For instance ' Biondello ' is the name for a fair-haired youth and the characteristics of Italian cities and districts are summed up with marvellous skill and correctness in a phrase. Lombardy is " the pleasant garden of great Italy." Pisa is " renowned for grave citizens," and so on.

(6) The betrothal of Petruchio to Katharina when her father joins their hands before two witnesses is an Italian custom.

Petruchio says : " I will to Venice to buy apparel 'gainst the wedding day," and we find that it was then the custom for gentlefolk to buy their wedding garments in Venice.

(7) From the passage :

" We'll show thee Io as she was a maid " and its context, Dr. Elze was confident that Shakespeare must have seen Correggio's famous picture of Jupiter and Io.

(8) The first act of *Othello* is thoroughly Venetian in spirit and atmosphere. The dark night, the narrow streets, Brabantio's house with close-barred doors and shutters, the low voices of Iago and Rodrigo, the sudden uproar, the torches and the " knave of common hire," the gondolier, etc., all this is a marvellous picture of a night in Venice, which could only have been drawn so surely and faultlessly from first-hand experience.

(9) Portia was obviously the true red-golden-haired Titian type found in Venice whose " sunny locks hang on her temples like a golden fleece."

(10) When Brabantio learns of his daughter's flight he calls for some " special officers of night." An extraordinary expression unless Shakespeare knew, as he must have done, that the night-watch in Venice bore the title " Signori di Notte."

(11) From the passage :

> 'Tis death for anyone in Mantua
> To come to Padua. Know you not the cause ?

it is clear that Shakespeare knew that Padua belonged to Venice and Mantua did not.

Mr. Brown says : " It was surely not a little for a London play-actor to know so much of the complicated political geography of Italy. . . ."

(12) The name of Gobbo is genuinely Venetian and suggests moreover the kneeling figure of stone, Il Gobbo di Rialto, that forms the base of the granite pillar to which, in former days, the decrees of the Republic were fixed.

(13) When Old Gobbo brings a dish of pigeons for his son's master he conforms to an old Italian custom.

(14) We may be a little surprised when Juliet says to Friar Lawrence, " Shall I come again to evening mass ? " but it is now known that there were " evening masses " in Italy in those days, especially in Verona, and there is a St Peter's Church, where Juliet was going to be married to Paris, on the Via San Fermo.

(15) In *The Winter's Tale*, Shakespeare praises the statue of Hermione as the work of Julio Romano. Critics, thinking that Romano was only a painter, have accused Shakespeare of blunder. We now know however that the poet was right and the critics wrong, for Romano was renowned in Italy also as a sculptor.

And so on and so on [1]—there is really no end to the quotations which could be cited, proving that Shakespeare's knowledge of Northern Italy was far too accurate and intimate to have been obtained second-hand. Shakespeare beyond a doubt not only visited Northern Italy, but remained there for some considerable time—perhaps a couple of years. He clearly knew the Italian language well and occasionally brought it into the text of his plays.

That either William Stanley, or Oxford, or Rutland, who all of them knew Italy and the Italian language, should base plays on the works of Italian dramatists and take their scenes from colourful Italian cities they knew so well, is natural and understandable ; but that Shakspere of Stratford, who had so feeble a background of education and culture should have used the works of Italian dramatists, of which there were frequently no English translations, is simply unbelievable.

---

[1] Professor Lambin's researches (see p. 113) show that Shakespeare had extremely intimate knowledge not only of Verona, Milan and Florence but also of Paris and the South of France.

CHAPTER II

OXFORD AND THE MAGIC CIRCLE

IN the last chapter we have seen that not only was Stanley in all probability at the Court of Navarre when Queen Marguerite was there with her *escadron volant*, but that his tutor Richard Lloyd was actually the author of *The Nine Worthies*, which is parodied in *Love's Labour's Lost*. I have also told how Stanley could have learnt the sad story of the death of Helen de Tournon, possibly from the lips of the Queen herself. It cannot therefore be denied that Stanley had the opportunity, the training and the education to enable him to write *Love's Labour's Lost* and the "Italian" plays, and that he alone of all possible candidates was personally associated with Richard Lloyd.

William Stanley returned to England not later than the middle of 1587. We will imagine that he brought with him the drafts of a number of plays in various stages towards completion. He was then about twenty-six years old and the first necessity for a young author, as anyone who has attempted to write a play knows well, is to find some person whose judgment he values to act as an audience and a critic.

But the plays were so packed with deep learning and matter relating to foreign lands that no one, who was not a scholar, a linguist, a courtier and a traveller as well as a poet, could possibly appreciate or criticise what he had written. In addition it was essential that his critic should know Italy really well. It would not therefore be surprising if Stanley submitted his plays to his kinsman Edward de Vere the 17th Earl of Oxford, who was recognised in his own generation as a poet and dramatist of very great merit.   Unfortunately if any of Oxford's dramatic works have survived, they are not recognised as his, and only twenty-five lyrics are actually known to have been written by him.

I have selected a few of Oxford's verses almost at random—and I think it will be agreed that they show a power of fine expression which is almost Shakespearean.

> If women could be fair and yet not fond,
>   Or that their love were firm not fickle, still,
> I would not marvel that they make men bond,
>   By service long to purchase their good will,
> But when I see how frail those creatures are,
> I muse that men forget themselves so far.
>
> And let her feel the power of all your might,
>   And let her have her most desire with speed,
> And let her pine away both day and night,
>   And let her moan and none lament her need,
> And let all those that shall her see
> Despise her state and pity me.
>
> What plague is greater than the grief of mind ?
>   The grief of mind that eats in every vein,
> In every vein that leaves such clots behind,
>   Such clots behind as breed such bitter pain.
> So bitter pain that none shall ever find
> What plague is greater than the grief of mind.
>
> If care or skill could conquer vain desire,
>   Or Reason's reins my strong affection stay,
> There should my sighs to quiet breast retire,
>   And shun such sights as secret thoughts betray ;
> Uncomely Love which now lurks in my breast
> Should cease, my grief by Wisdom's power oppress'd.

Born in 1550, Edward's mother was Margaret Golding, the sister of Arthur Golding, who, famous for his translation of Ovid, later became Edward de Vere's tutor.   From birth

Edward was surrounded by sporting and military traditions on the one side and by literary and classical interests on the other.[1]

His cousins were the famous fighting de Veres, Francis and Horace, and his tutor at Cambridge was Sir Thomas Smith. In 1562, when Edward de Vere was twelve years old, the 16th Earl died and Edward, as 17th Earl of Oxford, became ward of Sir William Cecil, afterwards Lord Burleigh, whose home was Cecil House. Edward took his degree at St. John's College, Cambridge, in 1564, and at the age of seventeen (1567) was admitted to Gray's Inn. Oxford was extravagant, arrogant and impulsive, spending lavishly on clothes, weapons, tutors and books. From bills paid on his behalf whilst still a ward at Court, we learn that he purchased—a Geneva bible, Chaucer, Plutarch's works in French, two Italian books and Plato's and Cicero's works in folio. In 1570 he served under the Earl of Sussex in a border campaign against the Scots Catholic nobles. Also in the same year he took his seat in the House of Lords and married Anne Cecil, Burleigh's daughter. Anne Cecil, from all one can learn, was a sweet and altogether charming girl—" an angel on earth." But Edward was far from a perfect husband, and maybe the affection was mainly on Anne's side. It seems that he considered he had married beneath him.

Between 1570 and 1580 Oxford became a great favourite with the Queen, but was for ever asking to be given opportunities for distinguishing himself in war or, failing these, for leave to travel abroad. He was a wild, restless, touchy, quarrelsome young man, who dressed in clothes colourful and extravagant even for the Court of Elizabeth. He was highly skilled in the use of weapons, but at the same time a distinguished scholar and a poet. Failing to get leave to travel abroad, he departed without

---

[1] Several of the early plays of Shakespeare show the influence of Lyly. It is therefore noteworthy that Lyly was Oxford's secretary and manager of his troup of players—known as the " Oxford Boys." Arthur Golding studied Law at Inns of Court.

leave to Brussels, but was chased and brought back by the Queen's Messenger.

Finally he obtained leave from the Queen to travel and left England in January 1575. In March he visited Germany and Strasbourg. In May he reached Padua and spent about six months in Northern Italy, returning to London via Lyons and Paris in March 1576, being shipwrecked on his way home. Whilst he was away, on July 2nd, 1575, his wife Anne gave birth to a baby, Elizabeth de Vere, the future Countess of Derby. A rumour was spread by that intriguing schemer Lord Henry Howard that Edward was not the father of this child. Oxford returned to England in a savage temper and refused to see either his wife or his father-in-law. He separated from his wife and the bitter quarrel was not made up till Christmas 1581. Oxford in fact acted in a violent and irresponsible manner which was quite unjustifiable. Burleigh and Oxford were poles apart in temperament, Burleigh being cautious, prudent, wise and ambitious in worldly matters, caring nothing for drama and poetry and little for scholarship. Oxford was an enthusiastic patron of drama, an amateur actor, and soon became known, owing to apeing Italian clothes and habits, as the "Italianated Englishman." It must be remembered however, that the documentary records which survive of Oxford's life mainly exist in the archives of Burleigh, who clearly disliked him.

There is but little more germane to this issue to say of Oxford's life. Anne Cecil died in 1588 and Oxford married again probably in 1592. From 1586 onwards he was paid the very large sum of £1,000 a year by the Government, it is said (by Oxfordians), for altering or writing propaganda plays. But, if so, it has never yet been made clear which plays Oxford altered or why the Queen should pay him this "salary," which was continued till his death.

In 1586 Oxford was one of the commission of nobles who tried Mary, Queen of Scots, and also, as Lord Great Chamberlain, he was one of those who held the canopy over Elizabeth at the celebrations of victory in 1588. During the latter part of his life he lived very quietly in the " King's Place " at Hackney and died there in June 1604.

It is astonishing how closely the literature-loving nobles of that remarkable age were interlinked by marriage or by engagements to marry. The Tree, on page 41, is taken, with a few minor alterations, from Professor Georges Connes' book *The Shakespeare Mystery* and I beg to acknowledge my debt.

Most of the great nobles of the Elizabethan age were ardently devoted to poetry and the drama. Many patronised troupes of actors of their own ; in fact, by statute, actors were vagabonds and it was not possible for a company of actors to exist unless under the protection of a great lord. These troupes frequently toured the country, playing in the big towns and in the great houses of the aristocracy. Indeed private theatricals and frequent visits by the professional players formed a large part in the home amusements of the aristocracy.

Surely there can never have been in any land an aristocratic clique which possessed such an exalted standard of education and culture as the Elizabethan upper classes—Oxford, Edmund Spenser, Sir Philip Sidney, Sir Walter Raleigh, the 4th Earl of Derby and his sons William and Ferdinando, Rutland and Lady Rutland (Sidney's daughter), Southampton and Lady Pembroke (Sidney's sister), to mention but a few. And to this galaxy of talent must be added the towering figure of Francis Bacon, who was intimate with them all. We know astonishingly little about their private lives ; but they impress themselves on our imagination as picturesque, explosive, enthusiastic, impatient, creative, artistic individuals, very young and very much alive, living in a dangerous and exciting age. In 1588, for instance, shortly after the return of Stanley, the Armada sailed up the Channel and was defeated. Oxford fitted out a ship of his own and took part in the fray, and it is believed that William Stanley sailed with him. Drake and Raleigh were scouring the oceans, carrying on what amounted to a private and piratical war of their own. These great men, though some violent quarrels are recorded,[1] were mostly excellent friends and, as they met often at Court, were all well known to each other. They frequently visited each other's houses and Wilton House on the Salisbury Avon, the home of the Earl of Pembroke, was a favourite meeting place where the drama and poetry were the subjects of greatest common interest and entertainment. They were nearly all scholars and linguists and many of them also concealed poets. They spoke or read Latin and French with facility and some of them had good knowledge of Italian and Greek as well. It is my belief that it was by the interplay of wit, knowledge and criticism in this unique circle of brilliant individuals that the plays of Shakespeare were forged. It would account for the vast store of varied knowledge in the plays, the immense vocabulary, the polish and repolish of lines.

This would not mean that there were many Shakespeares, but it would mean that the combined wisdom of a group of out-standingly intelligent aristocrats, who met frequently, who had ample time on their hands, whose greatest relaxation in life was pursuit of the Muses, who themselves provided an adequate audience and the severest critics, led by one master mind, formed a group—a magic circle, without which the divine works of Shakespeare could not have come to their full glory. There have been many instances in the past of groups or schools of artists, and of scientists, and the Master of such a group not only leads but is inspired by his own efforts of leadership, by the enthusiasm of his own pupils, just as his pupils are inspired by the leader to reach heights far beyond the individual capabilities of any member.[2] It would be reasonable to guess that this

---

[1] There was a famous quarrel between Oxford and Sidney which started in a tennis court and nearly led to a duel.

[2] *E.g.* The groups for instance around Pasteur and around Raphael, or indeed around any modern research professor.

Showing the close connections by marriage and engagements between some of the Elizabethan aristocracy

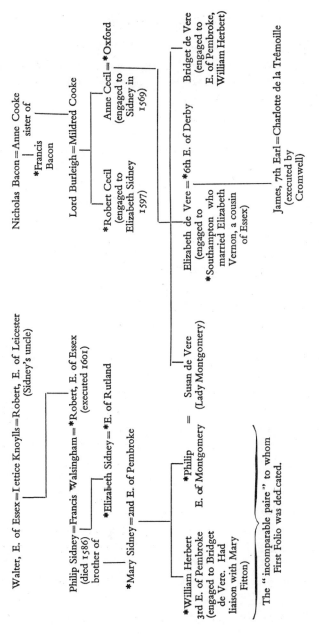

* Probable member of magic circle.   = Married to.

Shakespeare group started with the collaboration of Stanley and Oxford. Who contributed and how much the various contributions were ultimately worth is probably something which can never be known, but we do know that many of the plays were built on old material, and who can say through what stages they passed or who contributed a touch here and a line there before they were "alchemised" into pure gold by the mind of the Master.

In the same year that Stanley returned from the Continent, 1587, and, as I am supposing, read portions of his new plays to the Earl of Oxford, a troupe of actors under the patronage of the Earl of Leicester made the following long and interesting tour of the provinces : Dover, Canterbury, Oxford, Marlborough, Southampton, Exeter, Bath, Gloucester, *Stratford-on-Avon*, *Lathom House, Lancaster*, Coventry, Leicester.

They stayed at Lord Derby's House at Lathom and gave performances on July 11th, 12th, 13th, 1587.

Now 1587 is approximately the date when Shakspere of Stratford is supposed by tradition to have left his home town. It is really remarkable to find that Leicester's troupe travelled directly, according to the record, from Stratford-on-Avon to Lathom House. Considering everything, facts and tradition combined, it seems very reasonable to suppose that Shakspere joined up in Stratford with this troupe and came on with them to Lord Derby's House ; for, not many months later, on the death of Leicester, members of this same troupe came under the patronage of Lord Strange (Ferdinando) William Stanley's brother. Moreover Lord Strange's company subsequently (1594) became the Lord Chamberlain's company and it is to this company that Shakspere is known to have belonged in 1594 and for all his acting life. In view of this we may well ask who was the important and influential patron or protector of young Shakspere soon after he came to London. For it seems certain that Shakspere had some powerful influence behind him—more particularly someone who gave him money, for money he certainly obtained. Tradition says his patron was the Earl of Southampton, but the most profound researches of Mrs. Charlotte Stopes have failed to discover any connection whatsoever between Southampton and Shakspere the actor.[1]

Canon Beeching (the well-known Stratfordian scholar) when discussing the dedications to Southampton in *Venus* and *Lucrece* said: " If it be remembered that Shakespeare's patron, Lord Southampton, was one of the greatest peers in England, at a time when all social degrees, even that between peer and gentleman, were very clearly marked ; and that Shakespeare [Shakspere] belonged to a profession which, by public opinion, was held to be degrading, it will hardly need saying that such addresses from a player, however fashionable, to a patron, however complaisant, were simply impossible."

With this of course all of us fully agree, but Canon Beeching means that Shakspere was not just a protégé but a bosom friend of Southampton, which seems even more impossible since it is certain to have been unearthed by now if, by some miracle, it had been true. On the other hand, it does seem very possible that Shakspere was doing a job of work for the patron of his company, Lord Strange or his brother William Stanley, and was getting well paid for it. It seems therefore exceedingly likely that whilst Leicester's Company, in which Shakspere was employed in some humble capacity, was acting in Lord Derby's house in July 1587, that William Stanley came to know him. Perhaps the fact that their initials and Christian names were the same influenced Stanley in his choice of an agent or " Johannes factotum " as Robert Greene called the actor.[2]

[1] In her preface to the *Life of the Earl of Southampton*, Mrs. Stopes writes, " I must confess I did not start this work for its own sake but in the hope that I might find out more about Shakespeare." In this she was disappointed.
[2] See last pages of this chapter.
Note. That the poet's Christian name was Will (see Sonnet 136) is a very important point in favour of William Stanley, who later always signed himself " Will Derby."

Shakspere's duty would then have been, for a monetary consideration, to introduce on to the professional stage Stanley's plays and perhaps a number of alterations to old plays, even pretending that they were his own compositions. In which case the name and Christian name of his agent presumably gave Stanley the idea of adopting the excellent *nom de plume* of Shakespeare or, as it was often written, Shake-speare.

The name Shakspere has been spelt, we are told, in at least sixty-four different ways. As far as we can judge from the childish scrawls, which are " Shakspere's " signatures, the actor himself spelt his name " Shakspere," and, as shown by other phonetic spellings, it was certainly pronounced Shăckspur or Shaxper. Roche, the headmaster of Stratford, wrote the name Shaxbere (when he was referring to the actor's father). Abraham Sturley, a citizen of Stratford, wrote it Shaksper. Whittingham, the shepherd of Shottery, who lent money to Shakspere's wife, spelt it Shaxbere. The Court of Revels wrote Shaxberd. In the actor's will it is written Shackspeare. In the marriage indemnity bond it is Shagspere. Later, in documents concerning Shakspere's financial and real-estate operations, it is more frequently than not spelt Shakespeare. No one ever used the name " Shak-spere " with a hyphen, which makes Shake-speare so clearly a *nom de plume* and at the same time demonstrates exactly how it should be pronounced—Shake-speare ; not Shăckspur.

It was impossible for noblemen such as Oxford or Stanley to put plays upon the professional stage in their own names. The plays were primarily written either for the Court as Titherley suggested or for the edification of a circle of aristocratic and cultured friends—to be read and criticised in the group. They were most certainly not written for " Gain not Glory " as Pope vilely suggested, nor was their subtle philosophy addressed primarily to the public stage.

Many valuable opinions could be quoted on this point—
Swinburne expresses himself as follows :

" Of all the vulgar errors the most wanton, the most resolutely
tenacious of life, is that belief bequeathed from the days of Pope,
in which it was pardonable, to the days of Carlyle, in which it
was not excusable, to the effect that Shakespeare threw off
Hamlet as an eagle may moult a feather, or a fool may break a
jest . . . that he wrote 'for gain not glory,' or that having
written 'Hamlet,' he thought it nothing very wonderful to
have written. . . . Scene by scene, line for line, stroke upon
stroke and touch after touch, he went over all the old laboured
ground again ; and not to ensure success in his own day, and fill
his pockets with contemporary pence, but merely and wholely
with a purpose to make it worthy of himself and his future
students. . . . Not one single alteration in the whole play can
possibly have been made with a view to stage effect or to present
popularity and profit. . . . Every change in the text of ' Hamlet ' has impaired its fitness for the stage and increased its value
for the closet in exact and perfect proportion."

Sir Sidney Lee held a contrary opinion, for on page 503 of
his *Life of Shakespeare* he wrote :

Pope has just warrant for the surmise that he (Shakespeare)

> For gain not glory winged his roving flight
> And grew immortal in his own despite.

Such a view is not only an insult to our intelligence but a
gratuitous insult to the immortal Bard.

Orthodox opinions at one time differed as to how much of
Shakespeare's hand is to be found in *Henry VI*, Parts I, II and
III, but it seems to be agreed now that his hand is clearly visible
in all of them. In the latter part of *Henry VI*, Part III, it is
interesting to note that the Earl of Oxford is first introduced
and possibly it was the rewriting of the last three acts that
roused Robert Greene's ire.

From his deathbed in 1592 Greene wrote, warning three unnamed fellow writers, probably Marlowe, Peele and Nashe against " an upstart crow beautified with our feathers that, with his tygers heart wrapt in a Player's hide, supposes he is as well able to bumbast out a blank verse as the best of you : and being an absolute Johannes Factotum is in his own conceit the only Shake-scene in the country."

The words " O tygers heart, wrapt in a woman's hide " comes originally from *The Contention*, and is repeated in *Henry VI*, Part III.   Although his name is not mentioned, the use of the word Shake-scene makes it almost certain that this bitter accusation is against Shakspere ; not necessarily as an author— because " to bumbast out a blank verse " can mean to mouth verses as well as to compose them—though there would be little point in Greene, a writer, cursing Shakspere for acting. If, then, Greene was warning his fellow writers against Shakspere's boasting *pretensions* to authorship all that we are entitled to say is that Greene was accusing the player of putting forward as his own some blank verse of which he was not the author. In short, he accuses Shakspere of being an imposter, a Johannes Factotum, or agent for an unspecified dramatist.

The accusation was no doubt justified, but it is astonishing what importance is attached by the Stratfordians to this obscure and highly offensive reference to the Stratford actor. It has, *faut de mieux*, become one of the main pillars of the case in favour of the actor as author of the works of Shakespeare. But what a pillar!

From it the Stratfordians argue that already, even in 1592, the fame of the actor as a dramatist was known and the danger of his rivalry was recognised by the playwrights of the day!

CHAPTER III

OXFORD, DERBY AND HENSLOWE

FROM 1589 onwards Oxford, after having been a member of the commission which tried Mary, Queen of Scots, remained in retirement till his death in 1604. In 1588 he had a high reputation as a poet—for in that year Puttenham in his *Arte of English Poesie* said that a new race of poets, " Gentlemen in the Court," had arisen who had written excellently well if their names could be found and published, and followed with these words : " Of this number, the first is that noble gentleman, Edward, Earl of Oxford."

Oxford and Derby, already kinsmen and soon to be related by marriage, had in their education, in their lives and in their troubles, quite an astonishing number of similarities and common experiences. Both were scholars and linguists. It is probable that they could converse fluently in four languages, English, French, Italian and Latin. Each had had a University education, de Vere at Cambridge and Stanley at Oxford. They both, at different times, studied law at the Inns of Court. Oxford spent over a year abroad, partly in Northern Italy, returning to England in 1576, that is to say some years before the events occurred at the Court of Navarre on which *Love's Labour's Lost* is based. Derby went to France in 1582 and remained abroad for several years, travelling widely and spending probably two years or more in Italy before visiting Egypt and the Eastern Mediterranean and possibly joining Leicester in the Netherlands on his way home.

Both had great reputations for skill at arms and both fought duels in which they were wounded. Stanley's duel or duels are said to have taken place in Spain and some details are perhaps legendary. Oxford fought a duel with Sir Thomas Knyvet in 1582 in which both men were seriously wounded. Oxford had a considerable reputation as a musician and Derby was a musical enthusiast and even a composer, for in 1624 Pilkington of Chester published a Pavane for the Orpharion written by Derby—a pavane being a dance mentioned in *Twelfth Night*. Both Derby and Oxford had at different times been patrons of troupes of professional players and both were apparently enthusiastic amateur actors. It is a fact that the professional companies visited the Derby Mansions in Lancashire more frequently during 1590 than any other house belonging to any of the great nobles.

Largely through his own extravagance, Oxford was in grave trouble over money and had to raise it by selling many of his estates far below their real value. Derby, from the moment he succeeded to the earldom in 1594 and for ten years and more afterwards, was weighed down by lack of money, arising from litigation concerning the 5th Earl's will. The fortunes of the House of Derby at one time seemed to be in danger.

Oxford was without question a lyric poet of great merit, as we can judge from some of his verses already quoted. That Derby was a poet we know from the W. S. poems identified by Titherley and from Spenser's reference to Ætion in *Colin Clouts Come Home Again*,[1] and that he was also a playwright we know because in 1599 Fenner, a Jesuit spy, reported that Derby was only interested in " penning Comedies for the common players." [2]

During the Wars of the Roses the ancestors of both Derby and Oxford had been strong supporters of the House of Lancaster and in the plays *Henry VI*, Part III, *Richard II* and *Richard III* we find that the importance of the rôles played by their forebears

[1] See Allusion 7 Ch. VI.
[2] See two letters in the archives of Queen Elizabeth, both dated June 30th, 1599. Nos. 34 and 35, Vol. 271.

are emphasised unduly, certainly beyond what can be found in either Hall or Holinshed. For instance in the last scene of *Richard III* it is Lord Stanley who places the crown on Richmond's head, whilst the other nobles merely stand round in silence.

Neither Oxford nor Derby were happy in their relations with women. At least it may be said that they both showed a great deal of jealousy and suspicion in their married lives, and, as far as we can judge, without just cause. Both Oxford and Derby had first-hand experience of war on land. Oxford took part in a border expedition against Scotland in 1570. Derby was due to accompany Essex on his ill-fated expedition to Ireland in 1599, and was certainly a military expert. We hear of him reviewing troops and constructing fortifications in the Isle of Man. Both Oxford and Derby, especially the latter, took great interest in magic, astronomy and astrology. Thus the famous Dr. John Dee, astrologer to the Queen, was Derby's friend and protégé and near neighbour in Lancashire, and was also well known to Oxford. Dee, in his diary, notes frequent occasions on which he met Lord Derby or dined with him in Lancashire and London.

The practice of writing in collaboration was very common among dramatists in Elizabethan days. For proof of this it is only necessary to turn to Henslowe's Diary on which a short digression is necessary.

Philip Henslowe, in partnership with his son-in-law the actor Edward Alleyn, seems to have been joint owner or manager of several theatres including the Rose Theatre, Bankside, in which some of the early Shakespeare plays were performed. From 1591 to 1609 Henslowe kept a diary of the plays which he purchased and of the money he paid out or received from them. The names of nearly all the well-known dramatists of the day appear frequently in this large MSS. folio volume. It is a very remarkable fact that quite a number of the plays which

Henslowe bought and sold had names similar to the titles of the Shakespeare plays, so that it is difficult to believe there is no connection between them. For instance let us take the following records in his diary. Henslowe's spelling is phonetic and semi-literate.

(1) " R'd at Titus and Ondronicus the 23 of Jenewary (1593) III " VIII^s " ($£$3. 8. o.);

(2) " Re'd at King Leare the 6 of Aprell 1593 XXXVIII^s " (38/-);

(3) " 11 of June 1594 R'd at the tamynge of a Shrowe IX^s " (9/).

The dates given are the dates on which apparently these plays *Titus Ondronicus*, *King Leare* and *The Tamynge of a Shrewe* were performed in public.

But what are these plays and who wrote them ? The modern Stratfordians deny that the last two were written by Shakespeare, but then nowhere in the whole of Henslowe's diary is there one mention of Shakspere or Shakespeare. Yet we are told by Sir Sidney Lee that " The Rose Theatre " (owned by Henslowe) was " doubtless the earliest scene of Shakespeare's pronounced successes alike as an actor and as a dramatist."

Let us take some further extracts from Henslowe.

" Lent unto the Companye the 22 of May 1602, to geve unto Anthoney Monday and Mikell Drayton, Webster, Mydelton and the Rest in earnest of a Booke called Sesers Falle, the some of five pounds."

Is this Shakespeare's play *Julius Caesar* ? It was written apparently by four well-known poets " and the Rest."

Another entry from Henslowe runs :

" Lent unto Harey Cheattell and Mr. Dickers in part payment of ther boocke called Troyelles and Cresseda the 16 of Aprell 1599 XX^s " (20/-).

The two poets here mentioned are being authors of *Troilus and Cressida* are obviously Chettle and Dekker—both very well known. Shakespeare's play *Troilus and Cressida* was registered in 1603.

Again from Henslowe :

" Lent unto the companye the 9 of Novembr 1601 to pay Mr. Mondaye and Hary Chettle, in pt payment of a boocke called the Risynge of Carnowlle Wollsey, the some of X⁸ " (10/-).

Surely this must be a forerunner of *Henry VIII* ?

Stratfordians deny that any of these plays had anything to do with Shakespeare in spite of the extraordinary similarity of the titles. Are we really to believe that as soon as Henslowe purchased a play from some of the well-known dramatists of the day and produced it, Shakespeare immediately wrote a play of his own with almost exactly the same title ? We have in Henslowe's Diary probable references to the following plays : *Troilus and Cressida, The Taming of the Shrew, King Lear, Henry V, Henry VI, Titus Andronicus, Henry VIII, Julius Caesar, Richard II* and *Richard III*, but apparently all by other authors, not Shakespeare.

Henslowe's partner, Edward Alleyn, the famous actor, actor-manager, theatre owner and founder of Dulwich College, also kept memoirs, published in 1841, which their discoverer, Malone, says : " contain the names of all the notable actors and play-poets of Shaksper's [*sic*] time as well as of every person who helped, directly or indirectly, or who paid out money or received money, in connection with the production of the many plays at the Blackfriars theatre, the Fortune, and other theatres. His accounts are very minutely stated, and a careful perusal of the two volumes shows that there is not one mention of such a poet as William Shaksper in his list of actors, poets and theatrical comrades ! "

Furthermore, as Mr. Collier [1] tells us, between 1594 and 1596 for over two years, The Lord Admiral's players (in whom Henslowe was specially interested) and the Lord Chamberlain's servants, to which Shakspere belonged, were jointly occupying, or possibly playing in combination at the Newington Butts Theatre. During which period we learn from Henslowe that forty new plays were produced, among them a *Hamlet* and a *Lear* and a *Henry V* and a *Henry VI* and a *Taming of a Shrew*. Yet neither Henslowe nor Alleyn mention the name Shakespeare! And there are people who still say that there is not a Shakespeare problem! Once we try to accept Shakspere of Stratford as the author of the plays and poems there is just no end to the problems, difficulties and contradictions.

As already noted the touring companies of professional actors made very frequent visits to the houses of the great nobles, such as those of Derby, Oxford, Pembroke and many others. It was there I think that alterations were first made and scenes rewritten not only by Derby but by others of the fore-mentioned groups of enthusiastic amateur dramatists. Perhaps copies of some of the favourite plays (thus altered) were retained for private theatricals or more probably " readings " after the departure of the players. At first tentatively and with great caution the rewritten scenes began to be used by the professional actors on the public stage. We see in *Hamlet* how the great lord, the patron of the troupe, asks the players whether they could memorise and introduce into the selected play " some dozen or sixteen lines " of his own composition. Here we have, I think, a clear indication of how plays gradually underwent alteration. In due course these old plays, altered almost beyond recognition, with new thoughts, new knowledge and new words, came finally under the hand of the Master, and became known as plays by William Shake-speare. That is my theory, but it certainly seems extraordinary, if this hypothesis is approximately true, that Drayton, Dekker, Chettle,

[1] Mr. J. Payne Collier who edited and indexed Henslowe's Diary.

Munday, and other playwrights of the time should not have raised serious objections.

One can only reply that this toleration was reciprocated.

Numerous plays written by lesser poets appeared with the name of Shakespeare or W. S. on the title page. For instance :

Locrine. 1595. By W. S.
Sir John Old Castle. 1600. By William Shakespeare.
The London Prodigal. 1605. By William Shakespeare.
The Widow of Watling Street. 1607. By W. S.
A Yorkshire Tragedy. 1608. By W. S.

It is generally agreed that Shakespeare had no hand in any of these plays.

It seems to have been the intention of Shakespeare and his circle to incorporate into the plays as much collective knowledge as they possessed—that is to say almost all the knowledge which existed in England in that day. They were not so much interested in plots, but rather in Plato and Aristotle, in philosophy, philology, science, falconry, horsemanship, duelling, alchemy, magic, law, mythology and above all the reactions of human nature in the most tragic and trying circumstances. It will be noted that there were two extremely accomplished women in the " magic circle." Lady Pembroke and Lady Rutland— respectively the sister and the daughter of Sir Philip Sidney.

But of all the " magic circle," apart from Oxford and Derby, by far the most important was surely Francis Bacon. Bacon was one of the most widely learned and the most deeply cultured Englishman who has ever lived. He was Burleigh's nephew and in all the trouble and difficulties which arose between Burleigh and his ward, Oxford, Bacon must have been frequently consulted because Anne Cecil, the first Lady Oxford, was Bacon's cousin. He also took an active part in advising the commission which the Queen and later James I appointed to settle the great lawsuit which so gravely disturbed ten or more years of Derby's life. In fact he knew all the conceivable members of the " Magic Circle " intimately. To imagine that the revision and criticism of these plays, the insertion of new words, new thoughts and philosophy, law and science into them could have been accomplished without his knowledge and co-operation is, to me at least, incredible. He must have taken a part, and his mind was of such a quality and so well stocked and ready that it could not have been a small part. If so, to this extent the Baconians are right—that Bacon was responsible for much of the thought, the knowledge and the philosophy in many of the plays. As will be seen in Chapter VIII, I think it was partly to Bacon's initiative that we owe the production of the First Folio.

No doubt it will be said that the suggestion that numerous pens have assisted in the plays of Shakespeare is absurd. Stratfordian scholars, though frequently differing among themselves, claim to recognise the hand of the Master in almost any phrase. The tendency lately among the scholars is to attribute to Shakespeare alone everything or nearly all that is to be found in the First Folio and to reject, as far as possible, the idea that other pens participated in any of the plays. But many critics have thought otherwise. Dr. Garnett,[1] for instance, in the course of a lecture to the London Shakespeare Society, said : " It may surprise some of my hearers to be told that so considerable a part of the work which passes under Shakespeare's name, is probably not from his hand." (Lecture, April 14th, 1904.) J. M. Robertson, in his book *The Genuine Shakespeare*, 1930, contends that very large proportions of many of the plays were not written by Shakespeare.

[1] Garnett, Richard and Gosse, Edmund. *English Literature : An Illustrated Record.* 2 vols. 1903.

CHAPTER IV

DERBY AND *MIDSUMMER NIGHT'S DREAM*

IN 1594, the 5th Earl of Derby died, and William Stanley succeeded to the title. According to rumour, William's marriage to Elizabeth de Vere was postponed till it was known what the sex of the 5th Earl's posthumous child would be. It was said to have been a girl.[1] At all events, on January 26th 1595, Derby and Elizabeth de Vere were married at the Royal Palace of Greenwich in the presence of the Queen and her Court and it is probable that Edward Russell, Earl of Bedford and Lucy Harington were married at the same time. From Oberon's last speech in *Midsummer Night's Dream* it would appear that three couples were married on that occasion, though we know of only two.

> *Oberon :* Now, until the break of day,
> Through this hour each fairy stray,
> To the best bride-bed will we,
> Which by us shall blessed be ;
> And the issue there create
> Ever shall be fortunate.
> So shall all the couples three
> Ever true in loving be :
>
> (Act V, Scene II)

According to Sidney Lee and Chambers *A Midsummer Night's Dream* was written to be played before the Queen and her Court as part of the festivities of this marriage.

[1] See p. 60 for cause of postponement of the Derby marriage. According to Dr. Titherley there is no record of the birth of this daughter. William Stanley was recognised as the 6th Earl immediately after his brother's death. But if Alice, the 5th Earl's wife, had given birth to a boy, then the boy would have been the rightful heir to the title. It seems possible that the story that the Dowager Countess of Derby was enceinte was put up as an excuse for the postponement of the Derby–Elizabeth de Vere marriage.

As there is no record of payment for this performance it is probable that the bridegroom settled the bill. The actors were from the Lord Chamberlain's Company—the company to which Shakspere of Stratford belonged and which had been under the patronage of the 5th Earl of Derby till his death nine months before William's marriage, but there is no record as to whether or not Shakspere of Stratford was one of the actors in this performance.

Now Chester, Derby's favourite town, to which he retired in his old age, was noted for the Whitsun and Midsummer " shows " which are such remarkable examples of the popularity of acting in sixteenth-century England. For half a century the Derby family had taken the greatest interest in these Chester pageants and festivities, as for instance in the production of *Æneas and Dido* in 1563, which was attended by the 3rd Earl of Derby and his son, the father of our William. There are many similar instances, and in 1564 a banquet was given to Lord Derby " the weake after Midsomer." As Lefranc said :

(Translated): " One sees from this how closely the House of Derby was associated with Midsummer festivities at Chester." There is little doubt that this play, *Æneas and Dido*, is the same as that from which the touring players in *Hamlet* deliver a speech at Hamlet's request. William would have been but three years old in 1564, but there is no reason why this play *Æneas and Dido* should not have been repeated at Chester in later years as others were. In 1577, there was a brilliant presentation of the Whitsun plays at Chester. " The sheappardes playe " was played at High Cross. From *The Digby Mysteries* published by the New Shakespeare society in 1882, we learn :

" 1577. Alsoe (the Mayor, Thomas Bellin) caused the Sheappeardes playe to be played at the hie Crosse, with other Triumphes one the Roode Deey " . . . and the Mayor " enterteyned the Earl of Darbie and his sonne Ferdinando, Lord Strange two nightes at his howse " . . . " the scollers of the freescole also played a comedy before them at Mr. Maior's howse."

There are two explicit references in Shakespeare's works to the Whitsun plays.

The earliest is *Two Gentlemen of Verona*, Act IV, 4.

> *Sylvia.* How tall was she ?
> *Julia.* About my stature : for at Pentecost
> When all our Pageants of delight were played, etc.

The second reference is in one of the last Shakespeare plays— *The Winter's Tale*, Act IV, 3.

> *Perdita.* Methinks I play as I have seen them do
> In Whitsun pastorals :

From Robert Rogers, who in 1609 gave an account of these pageants and festivities at Chester, we learn that in some years religious plays and pageants took place both at Whitsun and Midsummer, but the Midsummer pageants continued after the more popish Whitsun plays had ceased.

It appears that each artisan guild produced its own play and Lefranc has shown that the inner play in *Midsummer Night's Dream* is a skit, but by no means unkindly skit, on the laboured efforts of these amateur artisan actors. No doubt the title *A Midsummer Night's Dream* means a memory of Midsummer plays produced yearly at Chester, and Bottom, the weaver, Quince, the carpenter, Snug, Flute, Snout, Starveling are pure types of the Chester workmen who gave crude performances there yearly as part of the Midsummer pageants.

Theseus, the Duke of Athens, introducing these very amateur actors, whose patron he is, to Hyppolyta, is, according even to the orthodox Chambers, Lord Derby himself presenting the Chester artisan actors to his bride Elizabeth de Vere. Perhaps Elizabeth had expressed some doubt as to whether it was kind to ridicule the crude efforts of the Chester workmen. One can

well imagine that Derby had given her a humorous description
of the Midsummer pageants.

To such a doubt Shakespeare gives the perfect answer :

Philostrate. A play there is, my lord, some ten words long,

.   .   .   .   .   .

There is not one word apt, one player fitted.

.   .   .   .   .   .

Which when I saw rehearsed, I must confess,
Made mine eyes water ; but more merry tears
The passion of loud laughter never shed.

Theseus. What are they that do play it ?

Philost. Hard-handed men, that work in Athens here,
Which never laboured in their minds till now,
And now have toil'd their unbreath'd memories
With this same play, against your nuptial.

Theseus. And we will hear it.

Philost.   No, my noble Lord ;
It is not for you : I have heard it over,
And it is nothing, nothing in the world ;
Unless you can find sport in their intents,
Extremely stretch'd and conn'd with cruel pain,
To do you service.

Theseus.   I will hear that play ;
For never anything can be amiss,
When simpleness and duty tender it.
Go bring them in : and take your places, ladies.

Hippolyta. I love not to see wretched men o'ercharged.
And duty in his service perishing.

Theseus. Why, gentle sweet, you shall see no such thing.

Hippolyta. He says they can do nothing in this kind.

Theseus. The kinder we, to give them thanks for nothing.
Our sport shall be to take what they mistake :
And what poor duty cannot do, noble respect
Takes it in might, not merit.

Midsummer Night's Dream, to a marked degree, like *Hamlet*,
or indeed almost any other Shakespeare play, is in tone aristocratic throughout. In this play there are numerous unmistakable
references to the brilliant festivities in the honour of the Queen

given by the Earl of Hertford at Elvetham in 1591. For instance, at Elvetham where Auberon figured as a fairy King, the Queen was enthroned at the west end of the lake—" a fair vestal throned by the west." At the banquet the sweets included whales, dolphins and mermaids moulded in sugar ; one piece of confectionary perhaps showing " a mermaid on a dolphin's back." At night the display of fireworks were surely responsible for Oberon's words " and certain stars shot madly from their spheres." In the opinion of Chambers, confirmed by Titherley, it was at this fête that William Stanley fell in love with Elizabeth de Vere, who was one of the Queen's maids of honour. In fact the whole play contains intimate records of Derby's life, being full of allusions which could have been understood only by an aristocratic audience, many of whom had also been present at the Elvetham fête and knew something of Derby's love romance. It is obviously impossible that a commoner like the Stratford actor could have been present in 1591 at these festivities, which were solely attended by the aristocracy. Surely *Midsummer Night's Dream* must have been written by Derby himself as a charming wedding present to his bride.

Certain allusions to the Queen in this play are so daring, as well as complimentary, that only an aristocratic author of the highest rank, and one specially in the royal favour, could have presumed so far. A bridegroom is a privileged man on the night of his wedding ; but even so the following are very bold lines.

OBERON TO PUCK

Oberon. That very time I saw, but thou could'st not,
Flying between the cold moon and the earth,
Cupid all arm'd : a certain aim he took
At a fair vestal, throned by the West,
And loos'd his love-shaft smartly from his bow,
As it should pierce a hundred thousand hearts ;
But I might see young Cupid's fiery shaft
Quench'd in the chaste beams of the wat'ry moon,

And the Imperial votaress passed on,
In maiden meditation, fancy-free.
Yet mark'd I where the bolt of Cupid fell :
It fell upon a little western flower,
Before milk-white, now purple with love's wound,
And maidens call it, Love-in-idleness.
                    Midsummer Night's Dream,
                    Act II, Scene I.

The probable interpretation of these lines was originally suggested by Mr. Lucas.[1] Lord Derby, when he succeeded to the Earldom, was the most eligible bachelor in England and there are indications that he was considered by the Queen as a possible Consort. This is by no means an impossible supposition, for Derby was thirty-three years old in 1594 and by his descent from Henry VII through the female line was strictly the only legal pretender to the throne. His tolerance of Catholicism might well have prevented a dangerous situation on Elizabeth's death, so that such a marriage would have been a wise act of statesmanship. Lastly there is that peculiar postponement of Derby's marriage with Elizabeth de Vere, for which there is no other satisfactory explanation. Was there a pause for several months in 1594 whilst the Queen was considering the matter before rejecting Derby as a consort ?[2] If these are the hidden facts how superbly the lines fit them. What a delicate and tactful compliment Derby paid to the Queen, flattering her virginal pretensions and emphasising the strength of her resistance to Cupid's love-shaft loos'd " as it might pierce a hundred thousand hearts." With this interpretation Derby's bride, Elizabeth de Vere, would be the " little western flower " on whom Cupid's love-shaft fell after missing the Queen.

Lord Derby's marriage does not seem to have been an entirely happy one. At any rate, in their early married life peaceful times were intermittent, and when Lady Derby died they were

---

[1] Macdonald Lucas in *Shakespeare's Vital Secret.*
[2] See Allusion 10, Ch. VI.

living apart. At one time certainly, Derby suspected his wife of
an affair with Essex, and Lady Derby may equally have had
doubts about her husband's friendship with Mary Fitton. It is
interesting to note that for a long time the Stratfordians believed
that Mary Fitton was the " dark lady " of the sonnets, in spite
of the fact that her portraits show her to have been fair. Sir
Edward Fitton and his daughter Mary were close friends and
neighbours in Lancashire of the Derby family and frequently
visited Knowsley. Thus it is possible that the tradition that
Shakespeare had some liaison with Mary Fitton has a basis in
fact, though the Stratfordians never seem to have considered
how absurd it was to imagine, even for a moment, that the
actor Shakspere could have been Mary Fitton's lover. In 1597
William, the son of the 2nd Earl of Pembroke, was urged by his
family to marry Bridget, the Earl of Oxford's daughter, and
thus become Derby's brother-in-law ; but Pembroke resisted
the proposal and instead became Mary Fitton's accepted lover
and had a child by her in 1601, when he was 3rd Earl of Pembroke. Other points of interest in Derby's life may be now
briefly touched upon :

On August 22nd, 1597, Lord and Lady Derby stayed at
Alport Lodge, Manchester, where he renewed acquaintance with
John Dee (the famous magician-mathematician), a meeting which
John Dee noted in his diary. Another friend of the Derby
family was Thomas Lodge, who, as the 4th Earl's protégé was
known to William from childhood and as a colleague at Lincoln's
Inn ; for when, on Derby's elevation to the Earldom, Lodge
dedicated his book, *A Fig for Momus*, to the new Earl, he
describes himself as " of Lincoln's Inn gent." It was from
Thomas Lodge, well known as a playwright, that Shakespeare
borrowed part of the plot of *As You Like It*, following the
main conventions of Lodge's *Rosalynde* with great fidelity, but
adding a freshness and vitality as well as several entirely original
characters—Jacques, Touchstone and Audrey.

In May and June of 1599 Derby was living with his wife in retirement in a cottage at Castle Hedingham, and it was there, as I have previously mentioned, that the Jesuit agent Fenner found him " interested only in writing comedies for the common players." Fenner's letters were intercepted by Elizabeth's counter-espionage organisation and were discovered by James Greenstreet in 1891.

In 1600, Derby's uncle, Sir Thomas Stanley, died and it is no doubt rightly believed by Shakespearean scholars that Shakespeare wrote his epitaph in Tong Church.[1] In 1598 Derby was compelled to sell a very large amount of land to raise money, because, owing to the lawsuit, he had grave difficulties in obtaining sufficient money to run his vast estates and keep up his establishments.[2] In the same year he wrote a letter to Sir Robert Cecil asking him to use his influence to obtain mercy for an unfortunate young man condemned to be hanged for stealing a silver spoon. On April 23rd, 1601, the Order of the Garter was conferred upon Derby and the investiture took place on May 26th of the same year. In 1602 there was a Star Chamber action brought by a Stephen Proctor against the agents of Lord Derby for deer stealing and other violent offences.[3] On December 2nd, 1606, Derby wrote to the Mayor of Chester asking him to give a good welcome to a touring company of actors under the patronage of Lord Hereford. He tells the Mayor that these players would be coming on later to play before him at Lathom. In 1608 Derby reviewed seven hundred soldiers about to leave for Ireland and gives a report of their poor condition. In 1607 his eldest son James, later known as the Great Earl of Derby, was born. In 1609 Derby's historic title as King of the Isle of Man was confirmed by King James I.

[1] See Allusion 14, Ch. VI.
[2] The *Merchant of Venice* was written about 1596 when Derby was already becoming oppressed by financial troubles.
[3] See Ch. VII, p. 110.

In 1617 James I stayed with Derby at Lathom House and in the same year Derby was made a councillor of Wales. Also in this year James I authorised a far greater freedom for Sunday amusements, in Lancashire, probably as a result of a request by Lord Derby. In 1626 James I recognised Derby and his son James, Lord Strange, as joint Lord-Lieutenants of Cheshire and Lancashire. In the same year Lord Strange married Charlotte de Trêmoille. In 1627 Lady Derby died at Richmond, aged fifty-one.

About 1623 Derby retired to Chester and left to his son increasing power in the management of his great offices and estates. It was at Chester that his daughter-in-law, Charlotte de Trêmoille, visited him in 1627 and wrote to her mother, telling of the visit : " Je vous mandais, Madame, comme j'avais vu monsieur mon beaupère, en une ville la principale de Chester, ou il demeure continuellment, ne voulant aller en aucune de ses maisons, il y a déjà trois ou quatre ans : il me parle français et me dit force obligeantes pâroles, m'appelant dame et maitresse de la maison, qu'il ne voulait point d'autre femme que moi et que j'avais tout pouvoir."

It will be noted that the approximate date of Derby's retirement was also the date of the publication of the First Folio.

The Earl of Derby died at Chester on September 29th, 1642, at the age of about eighty-one, having taken so little interest in politics that, in the *Dictionary of National Biography*, there is nothing to be found about his life. For the very little that I have recorded here of his life I am largely indebted to Professor Abel Lefranc's book, *Sous le Masque de William Shakespeare*.

CHAPTER V

SOME MEMBERS OF THE MAGIC CIRCLE

IN this chapter we will consider briefly some of the probable
members of what I have called the " Magic Circle " and to
discuss what parts they may have taken in the production
and publication of the plays of Shakespeare.

We have already seen how useful Rutland might have been
with his excellent library at Belvoir, his scholarship and his
knowledge of Italy. Moreover someone who visited Elsinore
after the publication of the 1603 quarto (QI) of *Hamlet* appears
to have provided Shakespeare with detailed information which
enabled him to make some interesting alterations in the 1604
quarto (QII). More Danish names are introduced. The name
Corambis for instance in QI is changed to Polonius in QII, a
latinised form of the aristocratic Swedish name of Plönnies, a
family whose members frequently took service with the Danish
crown.

The names of the two courtiers—written in QI as Rossen-
craft and Gilderstone are in QII spelt in the Danish manner
as Rosencrans and Guyldersterne. The innkeeper to whom
the gravedigger sends for wine, is unnamed in QI, now
becomes in QII " Yaughan," no doubt the anglicised spelling
of Jörgen.

In Act I, Scene I, the stage direction " a platform before the
castle " is found in QII but not in QI. But there is such a platform
at Kronborg Slot (Hamlet's castle). It is a stone platform
flanked by battlements where antique cannon still stand at their
embrasures. By the natives of Elsinore it is now known as the
" Ghosts' Walk."

In QI, Act I, Scene I, we have the lines :

> But look, the morn in russet mantle clad,
> Walks over yonder mountain top.

There are no mountains visible from the castle, but in the east there is one high hill, beyond the low-lying Swedish coast-line, which the rising sun would illuminate. In QII this has been noted and the lines changed to :

> But look, the morn in russet mantle clad
> Walks o'er the dew of yon high eastern hill.

And there are a number of other accurate details which prove that either Shakespeare himself had visited Elsinore or someone who had been there had reported to him. Now it so happens that James I sent an embassy to Denmark, with Rutland as ambassador-extraordinary, to attend the wedding of Christian IV's son and heir. With his attendants of knights and esquires Rutland sailed in the *Golden Lion* on June 28th, 1603, and landed at Elsinore on July 7th. The embassy was visited there by the Danish King and proceeded to Copenhagen. The King and Rutland conversed in Italian—their only common language. There is no mention of any Swiss guard in QI, but in Act IV, Scene V, QII, the King says :

" Where are my Switzers ? Let them guard the door." On the homeward voyage the embassy encountered a fearful storm. They could not put into Gravesend as they had intended and eventually landed at Scarborough on July 30th.

These details mainly taken from Mr. Sykes' book, *Alias William Shakespeare*, prove nothing, but they show that Rutland might well have been the source of up-to-date information about Elsinore and the Danish Court which caused Shakespeare to make some alterations in the 1604 quarto. There is also a great deal more in Mr. Sykes' book which shows that Rutland was closely associated with the plays of Shakespeare, but the foregoing is sufficient to indicate that if there was a " magic

S.M.C.—5

circle " around Shakespeare then surely Rutland was a member of it.

Rutland and Essex at one time seem to have been close friends and to have visited the theatre frequently together, so that Essex must also be included in the " Circle." There is that curious and so far unexplained episode in the Essex rebellion of 1601 when Shakespeare's *Richard II* was played many times in the streets as propaganda for the revolt—to the great indignation of the queen. After the arrest of Essex, Augustine Phillips, the manager of the Lord Chamberlain's Company (to which the Stratford actor belonged) was summoned before the commission appointed to try Essex to explain how this had been permitted. Obviously he faced a very serious charge of abetting treason ; but Phillips and the Players came to no harm. Apparently they were completely exonerated ; nor was the name of Shakspere the actor even mentioned ! How more than curious if he were the author of the objectionable deposition scene in *Richard II* ! This scene is the only portion of the plays of Shakespeare which is known to have been censored in the first quartos. Yet there would have been little purpose in playing *Richard II* to stir up rebellion unless this scene had been included. What unbelievable impudence on the part of the Players ! How could they have been exonerated ? The most likely answer was that Essex was alone responsible. As a member of the Magic Circle he would have been one of the " Grand Possessors " who controlled the plays of Shakespeare.

This term " The Grand Possessors," mentioned in the preface to the 1609 quarto of *Troilus and Cressida*, is extremely interesting. In the year 1609 two quartos of this play were published—an astonishing and inexplicable duplication. One of these quartos was introduced by a preface, which Malone and some other Shakespearean scholars of the past have, on internal evidence of both style and matter, attributed to Ben Jonson. It is a remark-able effusion somewhat resembling Heminge and Condell's preface to the First Folio which undoubtedly was mainly written by Jonson (see p. 129). I will not quote the whole of it. It starts :

" *A never writer to an ever reader.*

News."

" Eternal reader, you have here a new play, never staled with the stage, never clapper-clawed with the palms of the vulgar, and yet passing full of palm comical ; . . ."
An opening which is completely in Jonson's style. Later :
" It deserves such labour, as well as the best comedy in Terence or Plautus. And believe this, *that when he is gone, and his comedies out of sale you will scramble for them* . . ." (my ital.).

Note that the author of the preface speaks of the author of *Troilus and Cressida* as a living man in 1609.

Again :
". . . but thank Fortune for the scape it hath made amongst you, since by the grand possessor's wills I believe you should have prayed for them rather than been prayed." In other words the readers or theatregoers are lucky that the wishes of the Grand Possessors (that is the owners of the play) have not prevented the publication of this play. Who then were these Grand Possessors ? The Stratfordians say that they must have been Shakespeare's (Shakspere's) company. But such a term seems highly unsuitable for a troupe of actors.

Now when the First Folio was published in 1623, twenty of the thirty-six plays had never been published and of these six apparently had never even been heard of. Among the twenty were many of the greatest plays that have ever been written.

For the moment we will leave consideration of the mystery of the fourteen known but unpublished plays, for it is possible that there were copies of many of them in the archives of the acting companies. But the six unheard-of plays present a problem for which so far there is no acceptable explanation.

We are asked to believe that Shakspere of Stratford, who, by orthodox theory, wrote "for gain not glory," died with these plays unsold and unproduced and unpublished. Is it possible to believe that a keen business man like Shakspere, who in his "will" made such a meticulous distribution of his goods, would have made no provision for the sale or publication of these plays for the benefit of his heirs if he had really written and possessed them ? But, as noted, there is no mention at all of papers or books in Shakspere's will. Who then held the plays all these years and produced them when someone decided about 1621 to make a collection of the works of Shakespeare ? Sir Sidney Lee tells us that few if any of the Folio plays were printed from Shakespeare's autograph MSS. They were mostly taken either from the old quartos, or from prompt copies or from copies in private hands. Whose private hands we may well ask ? Who were the Grand Possessors of the plays with apparent authority to publish or not to publish the plays or even to conceal from the public the existence of a number of plays if they thought fit ?

The most likely "Grand Possessors" were the Shakespeare Society, which I have called the "Magic Circle." It is interesting to note that this preface was omitted from subsequent editions of *Troilus and Cressida*, so it may be that the words "Grand Possessors" endangered the secret as to the origin of the plays of Shakespeare. The person who was most likely to have been, what we should now call, the honorary secretary of the Shakespeare society was Mary, Lady Pembroke, Sir Philip Sidney's sister, and mother of the Earls Pembroke and Montgomery, to whom the First Folio was dedicated. She was certainly a remarkable woman, outstanding not only for her charm but also for her learning in days when the education of women in the upper circles in England was extraordinarily high. She was a prolific poetess, who wrote verses of much charm, learning and culture, though none which has survived even approaches Shakespearean standards. Numerous poets of the day praised her in verse—Thomas Nashe, Gilbert Harvey, John Davies, Edmund Spenser, John Donne, Ben Jonson among others. Daniel resided at Wilton as a tutor and dedicated his *Delia* to her. But it is as a friend and patron of poets that she most deserves to be remembered. Meres compares her to Octavia, the patroness of Virgil. She was born in 1561 and passed part of her youth in Kent and part at Ludlow Castle in Wales. She and her brother Philip Sidney were the closest friends, being both literary students and collaborators. They translated the Psalms together and *Arcadia* was written by Philip to her and for her and was corrected and published by her after his death.[1]

In 1577 she married the Earl of Pembroke and became mistress of Wilton, which henceforth was the " home of poetry " and the centre (as I believe) of the " Magic Circle." Ben Jonson was a frequent visitor ; Sir Walter Raleigh was a close friend ; in fact she probably saved his life in 1603 by her prayers to the King when he visited Wilton to see *As You Like It*. Queen Elizabeth probably visited her at Wilton in 1599. Surely Mary Countess of Pembroke had much of value that she could bring to assist in the revision of the plays of Shakespeare and to increase their richness. Being a Latin, Greek, Italian and French scholar Mary may well have had some part in swelling the fantastic vocabulary of the plays by anglicising French and Latin words and using them as Shakespeare so frequently did in their root meanings. Once that " game " had been started it must have been an irresistible attraction to scholars in the " Circle." More-over, as suggested by Slater, it is difficult to believe that there was not some feminine influence helping to form some of the characters and even some scenes in the plays. This is just a matter of taste and I do not wish to press it too hard. But would a mere man have written, " All the yarn that Penelope

---

[1] *Seven Shakespeares*, by Gilbert Slater.

spun in Ulysses' absence did but fill Ithaca with moths " ?   Then
the scene in Coriolanus when Volumnia, Virgilia and Valeria
gossip together as they sew was surely written or suggested by
a woman.   Even Goneril's irritation at Lear's undomesticated
habits in the house expresses strictly a woman's point of view,
and there is so much of the essential female in Rosalind and
Cleopatra for instance and in many other of Shakespeare's
women that it would not be surprising if a woman helped to
create them.   Then there is Shakespeare's familiarity with
Wales and his liking for Welsh characters which is so much in
evidence.   The Stratfordians have made the rather feeble
suggestion (as it seems to me) that Shakspere frequently came
in touch with Welsh shepherds who drove their flocks to the
Stratford market (if they did).   The followers of Derby point
to the fact that Chester, Derby's favourite town, was on
the Welsh border.   Certainly Shakespeare was very closely
acquainted with North Wales, but also he seems to be familiar
with South Wales, for many scenes in *Cymbeline* for instance
are laid near Milford Haven—a district which Lady Pembroke
knew well.   At Wilton Lady Pembroke collected a large library
in which there were many Italian books, her house being " in
a manner a kind of little court " with all possible members of
the " Magic Circle " as frequent visitors.

In 1603 she wrote a letter (since lost) to her son Pembroke,
asking him to try to persuade the King to visit her because " We
have the man Shakespeare with us."   Mary died in 1621—an
extremely interesting and suggestive date, because this was the
date on which Bacon was disgraced and fell from power.   Also
about that time Ben Jonson was working with him as a " good
pen " translating some of his books into Latin.   It is also about
the time that the first steps must have been taken to collect the
plays of Shakespeare for the First Folio.   If my theory is correct,
that the members of the " Magic Circle " were the " Grand
Possessors " of the many unpublished, including six unheard-of,

plays, and that Lady Pembroke acted as the secretary of this Shakespeare Society, then it is very reasonable to suppose that before her death she gave instructions to her sons for the publication of the plays. By 1621 few of the " Magic Circle " remained alive and the Earls Pembroke and Montgomery would have had really no alternative but to ask Bacon and Jonson to undertake the task of publication. We need not speculate as to the condition of these plays, because we know from the First Folio that many of them must have been in pretty poor shape. My suggestion is that their condition was caused by corrections, interlineations and even rewriting of some scenes by many hands.

To us nowadays it seems something of sacrilege that anyone should dare to correct Shakespeare—but I doubt if members of the " Magic Circle," poets and scholars themselves, looked at Shakespeare writings with the awe and respect that we do. They would think they were helping to improve the plays and maybe some of the richness and omniscience we find in them is due to their suggestions.

We may note in passing that the publishers of the First Folio were the Jaggards who had published four editions of Bacon's essays—a very natural choice if it was to Bacon that the " Grand Possessors " appealed for help. Once the First Folio had been issued it seems probable that, for security's sake, all these old MSS. were deliberately destroyed.

There is another member of the " Magic Circle," Sir Walter Raleigh, whose obvious usefulness to Shakespeare should be noted. Ten of the plays contain sea-storms which form an important part of the plot. We know that Oxford and Rutland both had experience of storms at sea—Oxford when he returned from abroad in 1576 and Rutland on his return from Denmark. Derby also must have had much experience of the sea and ships during his travels in the Eastern Mediterranean. But since all three were of course only amateur sailors how could they have had the professional technical knowledge which Shakespeare so

clearly possessed ? That Shakespeare had faultlessly accurate
technical knowledge of ships was confirmed by W. B. Whall
(Master Mariner) in his book *Shakespeare's Sea Terms*, 1910.
" Whoever wrote or edited the plays," says Mr. Whall, " had
an intimate professional knowledge of seamanship . . . and his
sea terms are always absolutely correct." Mr. Whall demonstrates this by scores of examples taken from almost every play.
He even suggests that Shakspere's knowledge of ships and the
sea is so profound that the actor may have been " pressed " into
joining the Navy during his lost seven years (1587–1594). It
has also been suggested by other Stratfordians that Shakspere
spent two years in an attorney's office and a few years as a
schoolmaster to account for his knowledge of Law and Latin.
Others are convinced that Shakspere obtained his intimate
knowledge of soldiering by accompanying Leicester's expedition
to the Netherlands in 1586. Lord Norwich even wrote a book,
Sergeant Shakespeare, to support this. And nearly all this time
the great plays were pouring out at the rate of two per annum,
many based on French or Italian backgrounds !

Mr. Whall states however that " in all the range of the Sonnets
there is not a single professional sea-simile. There are a few sea
allusions, but none which could not have been made by a lands-
man." The only exceptions are in Sonnets LXXX and LXXXVI.
Raleigh of course was a professional sailor and it is possibly to
him that Shakespeare owes his detailed accuracy in dealing with
ships and storms at sea. There are also many other passages
in the plays such as the mention of the anthropaphagi and the
cannibals and the " vast and idle desearts and high hills " in
Othello which may well have been derived from Raleigh's
experiences in distant lands.

Lastly, let us consider the 17th Earl of Oxford who, as already
shown, fits in so many ways my specification of the sort of man
who could have written the plays of Shakespeare. He was
recognised in his lifetime as a poet of the highest merit ; he

was a scholar, a linguist, a musician and a hunter, and I think it highly probable that he took an important part in rewriting some of the old plays, often with Shakespearean names, which we find in Henslowe's diary, originally written by other authors. That Oxford could have been an invaluable collaborator with Derby in the composition of many of the plays of Shakespeare can hardly be doubted. But there cannot be two Shakespeares and we must consider here the evidence which shows that Derby and not Oxford was the master mind of the " Magic Circle," the ". . . Alchemist which always had wit whose one spark could make good things of bad," as John Donne says in his sonnet addressed to the E. of D. and written about 1618.

In the first place, Oxford died in 1604 and there is strong evidence that the following plays were written after that date : *Macbeth, Coriolanus, Antony and Cleopatra, Timon of Athens, Winter's Tale, Cymbeline,* and *The Tempest.* The Oxfordians believe that first drafts of these plays were written before 1604 and that someone else finished them. *The Tempest* alone is a most formidable obstacle to this view and caused Mr. Looney to make the quite unacceptable suggestion that *The Tempest* was not by Shakespeare. It is unnecessary to enter this controversy because there are so many other reasons why Oxford cannot be Shakespeare.

Secondly, those of Oxford's lyrics which have survived, though very good, are not only not good enough but lack Shakespeare's majestic and flowing rhythm. Moreover there is in them not one spark of real humour or *joie de vivre.* They are written by an unhappy, frustrated man totally unlike the Shakespeare of the plays and long poems.

Thirdly, several writers, mostly protégés or friends of Derby, addressed Shakespeare, long after Oxford's death, as a living man.

For example, John Davies, in his epigram (see p. 94), written about 1611 to Mr. Will Shake-speare, uses the past tense in the first four lines, e.g., " Had'st thou not plaid some kingly parts in sport," etc., but in the last two lines changes to the present tense when he is clearly addressing a living man.

John Donne's Sonnet, already quoted, besides being addressed to E. of D., and almost certainly to Shakespeare, is throughout in the present tense and therefore to a living man. (Allusion 13, Ch. VI.)

The preface to *Troilus and Cressida* has a passage in the middle, as previously noted, which definitely shows that the author of the play was not dead in 1609. (67.)

Thomas Heywood in his *Apology for Actors*, 1612 (see p. 98, Allusion 12), says " the author I know [is] much offended with M. Jaggard," thus showing unmistakably that Shakespeare was alive in 1612.

Fourthly, Oxford's character, violent and quarrelsome, and his unchivalrous suspicion of women, which is a marked feature of nearly all his lyrics as well as of his known life, makes him quite unsuitable to be " gentle Shakespeare " or to have any important part in writing the lighter, more joyous or more fanciful plays—such as *Love's Labour's Lost, Twelfth Night* or *Midsummer Night's Dream*.

Fifthly, a very large number of corrections and improvements were incorporated in numerous plays long after the death of Oxford and also, some years after the death of Shakspere of Stratford. (See paragraph on *Merry Wives*, p. 109 *et seq.*) Most, if not all these revisions are accepted without hesitation by scholars as having been made by Shakespeare himself.

Sixthly and lastly, Oxford's name was Edward and not William or Will, nor were his initials W. S., which were certainly Shakespeare's as proved by *Willobie His Avisa*, and other contemporary evidence. (Titherley.)

CHAPTER VI

ALLUSIONS TO SHAKESPEARE [1]

IN this chapter we will consider a number of the contemporary references to Shakespeare or to some poet who may be Shakespeare and try to determine to whom they really refer. Of course the Stratfordians claim that all contemporary allusions to " Sweet Shakespeare " or " Gentle Shakespeare " etc., are necessarily references to the well-known actor who was playing at the Globe Theatre.

Quite lately a small book, *The Bacon–Shakspere Question* [2] has come into my hands. It is by C. Stopes—no doubt Mrs. Charlotte Stopes, the well-known and industrious Shakespeare historian. It was published in 1888. In Chapter IV, Mrs. Stopes gives a large number of allusions to Shakspere. But the greater number of these allusions are merely in praise of Shakespeare, and so signify nothing in respect of identity.

Until it is finally decided who Shakespeare really was, it is begging the question for one party to the authorship controversy to assume that all references to the poet, which give no guide as to who he was, were necessarily addressed to their candidate. Professor Lefranc might equally well have claimed that such references were addressed to Lord Derby, or Mr. Looney that they were addressed to the Earl of Oxford. I shall therefore omit those allusions which give no indication as to the identity of the author of the great works.

---

[1] For further discussion on these allusions see Titherley (*Shakespeare's Identity*).
[2] Note the spelling of the name Shakspere. It is only lately that " Shakespeare " has been officially adopted as the correct spelling.

(1) Some time before 1616 and probably between 1598 and 1604 Ben Jonson wrote a short poem which the Stratfordians, somewhat unwillingly, have accepted as referring to Shakspere. Jonson wrote very numerous poems of this description and called them epigrams. Epigram No. 56 is as follows :

> Poor Poet-ape, who would be thought our chief,
> Whose works are e'en the frippery of wit,
> From brokage has become so bold a thief,
> As we, the robb'd, leave rage and pity it.
> At first he made low shifts, would pick and glean,
> Buy the reversion of old plays ; now grown
> To little wealth, and credit on the scene
> He takes up all, makes each man's wit his own ;
> And told of this, he slights it.   Tut, such crimes
> The sluggish, gaping auditor devours ;
> He marks not whose 'twas first and aftertimes
> May judge it to be his, as well as ours.
> Fool ! as if half-eyes will not know a fleece
> From locks of wool, or shreds from the whole piece.

Since Shakspere's name is not mentioned one cannot be absolutely certain that these bitter words of Jonson were aimed at him. But as no one has been able to suggest any contemporary to whom they could apply with equal justice, and as the words " now grown to little wealth and credit on the scene " fit Shakspere, the actor, remarkably well, it is probable that they refer to him. It will be remembered that from 1597 onwards Shakspere had been buying real estate and had become a relatively rich man ; in 1599 he had purchased a Coat of arms and become a gentleman.

But that these lines should have been written by Jonson of Shakespeare the poet is difficult to believe, for *Venus and Adonis* and *Lucrece* had already been published, two scholarly and polished poems, which had received applause from a wide circle of cultivated men. Both poems were signed by " William Shakespeare " and as numerous editions had succeeded each other, Jonson was certainly familiar with them. Can we really imagine that Jonson wrote of the author of *Venus* and *Lucrece* in the scathing terms of this epigram ? It is impossible that so shrewd a poet as Jonson could have been guilty of such an absurd and ignorant error. By the lines :

> From brokage has become so bold a thief,
> That we the robb'd leave rage and pity it. . . .

Jonson indicates that a poet-ape who at first " would pick and glean " and make alterations to old plays, was now claiming larger works as his own. He makes it perfectly clear that he knows that these alterations were not the Poet-ape's own work and that such claims were crimes, which might deceive the " sluggish gaping auditor " but that " half-eyes will know a fleece from locks of wool or shreds from the whole piece."

Whatever Jonson's opinions may have been when he wrote this epigram, he must have retained them at least up to the death of the actor in 1616. For in that year he brought out a folio edition of one hundred and thirty of his epigrams, with a dedication to William, Earl of Pembroke, the elder brother of the " Incomparable Paire " to whom the First Folio of Shakespeare's plays was dedicated in 1623 and this poet-ape Sonnet is among these Epigrams (No. 56).

Jonson says in his dedication to Pembroke :

> I here offer to your Lordship the ripest of my studies, my Epigrams.

This " Poor Poet-ape " sonnet is so highly insulting that it is simply not possible to believe that Jonson and Shakspere were the best of friends and had frequent wit contests at the Mermaid. All that tradition must be sheer nonsense, for surely Jonson could hardly have uttered such an insult to a friend in the very year of his friend's death.

(2) Ben Jonson's play, *Every Man out of his Humour*, which is equally insulting, was first acted in 1599. This may be

approximately the time when Jonson wrote his "Poor Poet-ape" sonnet to Shakspere the actor. It is also shortly after the date on which the actor obtained his grant of arms with the motto *Non sanz droict*, and became a gentleman. It is not therefore very surprising to find that Jonson satirises Shakspere in his play in words the reverse of complimentary. He introduces Shakspere as an uneducated rustic called Sogliardo—which is the Italian for "a filthy fellow." In the first scene of the third act, Sogliardo, Puntarvolo and a clown called Carlo Buffone discuss the "Coat of arms" which Sogliardo has just acquired.

Sog.	Nay, I will have them, I am resolute for that. By this Parchment gentlemen, I have been so toiled among the Harrots (Heralds) yonder, you will not believe ; they do speak i' the strangest language and give a man the hardest termes for his money, that ever you knew.
Carlo.	But ha' you arms ? ha' you arms ?
Sog.	Y'faith, I thanke God I can write myself gentleman now ; here's my patent, it cost me thirty pound, by this breath.
Punt.	A very fair coat, well charged and full of armory.
Sog.	Nay, it has as much variety of colours in it, as you have seen a coat have ; how like you the crest sir ?
Punt.	I understand it not well, what is't ?
Sog.	Marry, Sir, it is your boar without a head rampant.
Punt.	A boar without a head, that's very rare !
Carlo.	Aye, and Rampant too ! troth, I commend the Herald's wit, he had decyphered him well : A swine without a head, without brains, wit, anything indeed, ramping to gentility—You can blazon the rest signior can you not ?

· · · · · ·

Punt.	Let the word be, "Not without mustard." Your crest is very rare, sir.

The above is undoubtedly an allusion to Shakspere and it is obvious that Jonson at this date despised and ridiculed him as an ignorant "clod." How is it then that Jonson so changed his mind that, in 1623, he wrote the magnificent ode to Shakespeare at the beginning of the First Folio ? The Stratfordians contend that Jonson was jealous of Shakspere. We heretics doubt whether this is an adequate reason—for it seems to us far more probable that Jonson knew perfectly well that Shakspere the actor was not Shakespeare the author. In fact there is no contemporary evidence whatever that anyone unambiguously identified the actor with the famous author. An oft-repeated Stratfordian argument is that, if the Stratford actor was not the author, the secret must have leaked out. Too many people, it is said, would have had to have been " in the know," and it is impossible that all of them would have kept silent. But if it is the case that no one, with the possible exception of Robert Greene, in 1592, ever thought that the actor had written a play or was capable of writing one—then, as far as the actor was concerned, there was no secret to be kept. There was certainly someone writing plays under the *nom-de-plume* Shakespeare or Shake-speare. But nom-de-plumes were common in those days—numerous plays and poems having appeared either under pen names or initials or anonymously—and no one ever bothered much to find out what was the real name of the author. No doubt those who considered the matter at all thought the plays and poems of Shakespeare were written by some concealed aristocrat, for no one but an aristocrat could have written the dedications to *Lucrece* and *Venus*. If for understandable reasons this nobleman did not want his real name to be known, that was his affair. This is shown clearly enough by the fact that when anyone referred to the author himself he invariably used the most obscure language. Few seemed to know who he really was and those few were mainly protégés of the House of Derby. If then one of the great nobles was the author of the Works of Shakespeare, the guarding of the secret presented no great difficulties at least up to the date of the preparation and publication of the First Folio in 1623, when the question had to be faced.

(3) *Polimantea*, by W. C. (probably either William Clerke or William Covell), was printed by John Legate, Printer of Cambridge University in 1595.

It contains a " Letter from England to her three daughters, Cambridge, Oxford and Inns of Court." W. C. alludes to writers of the University school, such as Spenser and Daniel and he has a marginal note :

> All praiseworthy Lucretia, Sweet Shak-speare.   Eloquent Gaveston
> Wanton Adonis.   Watson's heyre.

" Eloquent Gaveston " may be an allusion either to Marlowe from his *Edward II*, or to Drayton's *Piers Gaveston*, but " Wanton Adonis " must be an allusion to Shakespeare's *Venus and Adonis*. Watson's heyre (heir), Sir Sidney Lee thought, must be Shakespeare. Watson was a well-known writer of sonnets, whose patron was the Earl of Oxford, to whom he dedicated *The Passionate Century of Love*.

It is therefore of real interest to find that W. C. in this marginal note includes Shakespeare with University men like Marlowe and Watson and presumably also as a member of the Inns of Court.

(4) *The Return from Parnassus.*

We now come to an allusion to Shakespeare by name on which great store is set by the Stratfordians. It is in fact one of the three contemporary allusions, which alone might connect Shakspere as an actor with Shakespeare the author. The other two—Greene's death-bed accusation (p. 46), calling an unnamed actor an " upstart crow beautified with our feathers " and Ben Jonson's " Poor Poet-ape " epigram, we have already discussed. Neither of these mention Shakspere by name. Both are thoroughly unsatisfactory as evidence of Stratford authorship.

The Return from Parnassus or The Scourge of Simony was acted by the students of St. John's College, Cambridge, in 1601.

It was written apparently by a Cambridge student whose name is however unknown. The play is rather bitter and satirical but includes a passage making fun of professional players, where the author pretends to bring the two well-known actors,

Burbage and Kempe, on to the stage and puts into Kempe's mouth the following deliberate nonsense.

Kempe, Few of the University pen plaies well ; they smell too much of that writer Ovid, and that writer Metamorphosis, and talke too much of Proserpina and Juppiter. Why, here's our fellow Shakespeare puts them all downe, aye, and Ben Johnson too.

Oh, that Ben Jonson is a pestilent fellow, he brought up Horace giving the Poets a pill, but our fellow Shakespeare hath given him a purge that made him bewray his credit.

It is extraordinary that this ironical passage could have been taken seriously by anyone—it is so very obvious that Kempe is being mocked and laughed at as an ignoramus. He is allowed so little classical knowledge that he calls Metamorphosis a writer. He jibes at University pens because they talk too much of Ovid, Proserpina and Jupiter when of all poets surely it is Shakespeare against whom such an accusation might be most justly made.

"Why," Kempe goes on, "here's our fellow Shakespeare puts them all downe, aye, and Ben Jonson too," a remark which, put into Kempe's mouth by a University author, must be a withering sarcasm indicating that exactly the opposite is true. The players, Shakspere among them, are being held up to ridicule. What is meant by " our fellow Shakespeare hath given him (Jonson) a purge " has never been discovered. Sir George Greenwood suggests that it is an allusion to Dekker's *Satiro-Mastix*, in which there are many references to pills and purges to be administered to Jonson. Greenwood says :

" It is usually supposed that Shakspere took a part in it—some say of William Rufus—and in that sense " our fellow Shakespeare " may have taken part in administering the purge."

Satiro-Mastix, although not published till 1602, might well have been known to the Cambridge wits a year before.

It is abundantly clear that these remarks, given to Kempe by a university wit, are worthless as evidence that the Stratford actor wrote the plays of Shakespeare.

(5) In 1603, John Davies published his *Microcosmos*. This Davies is the same writing-master poet, a friend and protégé of Lord Derby, whose subsequent allusion to Shakespeare as " Our English Terence " I quote later in this chapter. (Allusion 10.)

	Some followed her by acting all men's parts,
	Then on a stage she raised in scorne to fall.
	And made them mirrors by their acting arts.
	Wherein men saw their faults though ne'er so small.
W. S. and	Yet some she guerdoned not to their deserts
R. B.	But other some were but ill-actors all,
	Who while they acted ill, ill stayed behinde
	(By custom of their manner) in their mind.
	Players I love you and your qualitie
Simonides	As you are men that pass time not abused
saith	And some I love for painting poesie,
Poetry is	And say fell Fortune cannot be excused
a speaking	That hath for better uses you refused :
painting.	Wit sharpe good courage good parts and all good
	As long as all these goods are no worse used,
	And though the stage doth stain pure gentle blood,
	Yet generous ye are in mind and mood.

The whole interest of this otherwise very uninteresting passage is the W. S. and R. B. in the margin opposite the line " Yet some she guerdoned not to their deserts." The Stratfordians naturally consider W. S. to be the Stratford actor and R. B. to be Richard Burbage, the well-known Shakespearean actor. They pick out the line " And some I love for painting poesie." As Burbage was also a painter it is contended that R. B. is referred to as a painter-actor and W. S. as a poet-actor. But unfortunately for this interpretation the remark of Simonides in the margin, " poetry is speaking-painting " makes the intended meaning perfectly clear. Namely, that an actor speaking poetic lines is, so to speak, painting a picture.

If, by the initials W. S. and R. B., William Shakspere and Richard Burbage were intended (as is possible but not certain), then the last two lines certainly cannot refer to either of them.

To say that the " stage doth stain pure gentle blood " in respect of a couple of professional actors with no pretensions to " gentle blood " would be utter nonsense.

(6) Edmund Spenser published Books I to III of the *Faerie Queen* in 1590, with a dedicatory sonnet to the Earl of Oxford among others. In 1591, he published *The Tears of the Muses*, dedicated to Alice, the wife of the 5th Earl of Derby, and the following stanzas in this poem are a source of controversy to this day :

> And he the man whom Nature selfe had made
> To mock herselfe and Truth to imitate
> With kindly counter under Mimik shade,
> Our pleasant Willy, Ah ! is dead of late ;
> With whom all joy and jolly meriment
> Is also deaded, and in doleur drent.
>   . . . (6 lines omitted) . . .
> But that same gentle spirit from whose pen
> Large streames of honnie and sweete Nectar flowe,
> Scorning the boldnes of such base-borne men,
> Which dare their follies forth so rashlie throwe,
> Doth rather choose to sit in idle Cell,
> Than so himself to mockerie to sell.

There are a few Stratfordians, Mr. Collier for instance, who have had no hesitation in claiming these fine lines of Spenser's to be an allusion to Shakespeare [Shakspere]. But these verses were *published in* 1591 and it is quite impossible to believe that the man of Stratford could, at that early date, have written anything to justify such praise—more particularly from Spenser, who was something of a snob.

As Sir George Greenwood says : " If this is an allusion to Shakespeare, as Collier and others affirm, it furnishes an additional argument in support of the contention that Shakespeare and Shakspere are not identical."

As we have seen, modern Shakespeare scholars have tried to date the plays as late as possible in order to give the Stratford actor a chance of educating himself before starting to write.

The claim that these words apply to Shakspere has therefore, with much regret, now been dropped by many Stratfordians. Sir Sidney Lee even suggested that they refer to a comic actor, Richard Tarleton, who had been dead three years, but this seems extraordinarily improbable for several reasons. Tarleton was a somewhat vulgar comedian and about the last man of whom the ultra-refined Spenser would have approved. Secondly, it appears from the stanza which begins : " But that same gentle spirit . . ." that " Our pleasant Willy " is not physically " dead of late " but figuratively so and having retired from writing poetry, " doth rather choose to sit in idle cell."

Professor Lefranc considered that these words referred to William Stanley and it is very tempting to the supporters of Derby to accept this. Mr. Looney claimed that these lines are an allusion to the Earl of Oxford. They might fit him well, because on returning from the battle with the Spanish Armada in 1588 Oxford did retire and from that time onwards nothing that he wrote was published under his own name. One of the difficulties in taking these lines as an allusion to Oxford is the name " Willy." Mr. Looney makes out a rather laboured case for the use of the name " Willy " as a reference to Oxford. Indeed in this he emulates Sir Sidney Lee, who has the same, or even greater, difficulties to overcome in suggesting that " Willy " means Richard Tarleton. A further difficulty for Looney's theory is Oxford's obvious lack of humour in his lyrics ; for Spenser's words " joy and jolly meriment " are quite out of keeping with what we know of Oxford's verse and character. Perhaps after all Lefranc was right in believing that " Our pleasant Willy " is simply an allusion to William Stanley. In this case not only is the name " Willy " correct but the word " Our " is quite natural in a poem dedicated to Stanley's sister-in-law (then Lady Strange) and written by Spenser, who was proud of his relationship with the Derby family. After the publication of *The Faerie Queen*, Thomas Nashe, in a letter to

Spenser, complained that he had omitted Ferdinando from his "catalogue of our English heroes, which insueth the conclusion of thy famous ' Faerie Queene '." He refers to Ferdinando as "Jove's Eagleborn Ganimed, thrice noble Amyntas." The appellation " Eagleborn," for a son of the Earl of Derby, should be particularly noted for it adds to the strength of the argument in the next allusion.

(7) The following lines from Spenser's *Colin Clouts Come Home Again* (written in 1591[1] and dedicated to Sir Walter Raleigh) are of outstanding interest to our quest for Shakespeare and are still the subject of endless orthodox controversy.

> There also is (ah no, he is not now)
> But since I said he is, he is quite gone,
> Amyntas quite is gone and lies full lowe,
> Having his Amaryllis left to mone.
> Helpe, O ye Shepheards, helpe ye all in this,
> Helpe Amaryllis this her losse to mourne :
> Her losse is yours, your losse Amyntas is,
> Amyntas, floure of shepheards pride forlorne :
> He, while he lived, was the noblest swaine,
> That ever piped on an oaten quill :
> Both did he other, which could pipe, maintaine,
> And eke could pipe himselfe with passing skill.
> And there, though last not least is Ætion,
> A gentler shepheard may no where be found :
> Whose Muse, full of high thoughts invention,
> Doth, like himselfe, heroically sound.

These verses were an interpolation written immediately after the death of Amyntas who, indisputably recognised as Ferdinando the 5th Earl of Derby, died in 1594, i.e., when William Stanley succeeded to the title.

The first twelve lines above are a funeral oration and belatedly fulfil Nashe's request. They appeal to other shepheards [*sic*] to help Amaryllis, Ferdinando's widow Alice, to bear her loss, which is also their loss.

---

[1] But not published till 1595.

In Spenser's long poem most of the real names of shepherds and shepherdesses are now well known.

> The Shepheard of the Ocean is Sir Walter Raleigh.
> Amyntas is Ferdinando, 5th Earl of Derby.
> Amaryllis is Alice, Ferdinando's wife.
> Astrofell is Sir Philip Sidney.
> Cynthia is Queen Elizabeth.
> Phillis ⎫
> Charillis ⎬ are Lady Strange's sisters.

The last four lines quoted above give the highest praise to Ætion, but who Ætion might be no one was able to discover until Professor Lefranc solved the problem in his book, *Sous le Masque de William Shakespeare*.

Sir Sidney Lee, in spite of some grave objections, claimed these lines to Ætion as an allusion to Shakspere (Shakespeare) and a good many Stratfordians, with some hesitation, have agreed. But throughout *The Tears of the Muses* and *Colin Clouts*, all the poets and poetesses mentioned were personally known to Spenser—and mostly were close friends of his. Spenser was seldom in London and careful investigation has shown it to be most unlikely that Spenser and the actor ever met. Whilst therefore it is reasonably certain that by " Ætion " Shakespeare is intended, it is quite impossible to accept these four lines as an allusion to the Stratford actor. Professor Lefranc has in fact shown beyond doubt, that they are an allusion to William Stanley, who, on the death of Ferdinando, became head of the house of Derby.

Ætion, as Lee says, is a familiar Greek name derived from Ætos, an eagle. The crest of the House of Derby is an eagle and a child. One of the Derby seats—Lathom House—is known as the Eagle's Nest, and the central tower is the Eagle Tower. In my opinion the head of the House of Derby and no one else could properly be called Ætion—The Eagle.

Whether from the lines :

> Whose Muse, full of high thoughts invention
> Doth like himselfe heroically sound,

and the use of the epithet " gentle," so constantly used for Shakespeare, we are justified in considering that Spenser thought Stanley to be Shakespeare—is a matter of opinion. It must be admitted that they fit such an interpretation remarkably well. Ætion's Muse—if taken as the *nom de plume* Shake-speare— certainly has an heroic sound and so has the name " Eagle " or Ætion, or for that matter the name Stanley in the history of England.

The first twelve lines quoted above are concerned solely with the House of Derby and were interpolated some time in 1594–5, after Ferdinando's death ; the last four lines starting : " And there though last not least is Ætion " and following immediately after, appear to have been added at the same time and it is natural and reasonable to take it that they also refer to the House of Derby—this time to the head of it.

It must be remembered that if there was a secret of authorship, it was extremely probable that Spenser knew it. Spenser, who was inordinately proud of his claim to relationship with the House of Derby, lived in Lancashire, the Derby county, between 1576 and 1578, and the house where he lived is still known as Spenser's House. He was a close friend of the Derby family and a great admirer of the three Spencer sisters—Amaryllis, Phyllis and Charillis of the poem being related to the Spencer family via Sir John Spencer, the father of the above three girls.

There is what appears to be an interesting cross-reference to *The Tears of the Muses* in *Midsummer Night's Dream*, a play which must have been written about the same time as the above-quoted addition was made to *Colin Clouts*, some time in 1594. It is in Act V, Scene I, where Theseus is choosing a play for the evening's entertainment and Philostrate suggests :

> The thrice three Muses mourning for the death
> Of learning, late deceased in beggary,

but Theseus rejects it as " not sorting with a nuptial ceremony."

(8) *Willobie His Avisa.*

In 1594 a very curious poem was published called *Willobie His Avisa or the True picture of a modest maid and of a chaste and constant wife.* This poem seems harmless enough ; nevertheless it appears to have been disliked by someone of influence because later editions of the poem were suppressed. It is probable that the line " And Shake-speare paints poore Lucrece rape " was the cause of the trouble ; maybe it was a key which, if used with local knowledge, might have unlocked a dangerous secret. Of the various attempts to interpret this poem that of Mr. R. M. Lucas in *Shakespeare's Vital Secret* is the most reasonable. His suggestions without being conclusive are extremely interesting.

The dedicatory Epistle is signed by Hadrian Dorrell who professes to have found the MSS. in Henry Willobie's room at Oxford. Whether Dorrell was a real person or not is of small importance. Perhaps the real author was Henry Willobie (or Willoughby) a native of West Knowle in Wiltshire, who was up at St. John's College, Oxford, in 1591. The poem tells how Avisa (first as a maid and then as a wife) is courted by numerous suitors and rejects them all. In due course we find an unsuccessful suitor, H. W., appealing to W. S. (" the old player ") for advice as to how best to overcome Avisa's resistance. W. S. himself had courted Avisa in the past—also unsuccessfully. Adopting a somewhat cynical attitude, he seems to enjoy watching H. W. enduring the same agonies of unsuccessful courtship as he had once suffered himself. All this has the appearance of being relatively harmless jesting by University students. Why then should Hadrian Dorrell take an immense amount of trouble later in 1596 to cover the whole affair with a veritable smoke-screen. He introduces an Apologia into the 1596 edition in which he says that the author, "now of late gone to God," wrote the poem thirty-five years ago—that is to say in 1561, which is obviously untrue. A date so far back would of course remove the poem from all contemporary interest, but does not in the least explain why some influential person objected so strongly to its publication that later editions were suppressed. He further suggests that Avisa is a name compounded of " A " and " Visa," meaning " not seen " (non-existent). Once we allow ourselves to become suspicious concerning this curious poem quite a number of suggestive points can be noted.

The first and obvious one is that the initials of the old suitor and the young suitor are W. S. and H. W. Can they possibly represent William Shakespeare and Henry Wriothesly (the Earl of Southampton) ? It should be remembered that Shakespeare had published *Venus and Adonis* in 1593 and *Lucrece* in 1594 ; the latter just before *Willobie His Avisa* was first issued. There is in the poem that reference " And Shake-speare paints poore Lucrece rape " previously noted and it is pretty clearly indicated that W. S. ("old player") is the author of *Lucrece*. This reference, the very first instance in which the peculiar hyphenated name " Shake-speare " appeared in print, together with the fact that W. S. is called " the old player " very naturally has roused the interest of the Stratfordians—but they are commendably cautious. Sir Sidney Lee says : " But Dorrell's protestations (his Apologia to the 1596 edition) scarcely carry conviction and suggest an intention to put his readers off the true scent. In any case the curious episode of W. S. is left without comment. The mention of W. S. as ' the old player ' and the employment of theatrical imagery in discussing his relations with Willobie, must be coupled with the fact that

Shakespeare, at a date when mentions of him in print were rare, was greeted by name as the author of *Lucrece* (' And Shake-speare paints poor Lucrece rape') in some prefatory verses to the volume. From such considerations the theory of Shakespeare's identity with ' W. S.,' Willobie's acquaintance, acquires substance." Mr. J. B. Harrison, a distinguished Stratfordian, goes much further : he, like other commentators, is of opinion that W. S. the cynical " old player," must be the author of the Shakespeare plays.

Nevertheless it is very hard to see how " old player " can possibly apply to the Stratford actor, who, though thirty years old, was only at the beginning of his career as an actor in 1594 when *Avisa* was published. He had quite definitely not retired from the stage, so that the allusion does not fit Shakspere ; nor does the University atmosphere of the *Avisa* poem. Nor, with William Shakspere the actor as W. S., has anyone been able to make sense of the poem much less to give adequate reasons for its suppression and for Dorrell's smoke-screen.

Let us then follow Mr. R. M. Lucas and, using our imagination, see what may result from making W. S. equal William Stanley and H. W. equal Henry Wriothesly, the young Earl of Southampton. In 1594 Derby was about thirty-three years old and the Earl of Southampton twenty-one. Let us eliminate Hadrian Dorrell and agree that Henry Willobie of West Knoyle, who was up at Stanley's old college, St. John's, Oxford, in 1591, was the author. St. John's was known for its enthusiasm for drama and " doubtless " William Stanley, when he was " up," took a very active part in the theatricals. He could therefore justly be called by Willobie " the old player " as far as the college was concerned. Furthermore, in 1594, William Stanley became the 6th Earl of Derby and we can well believe he renounced acting from that time on, as he would very naturally consider acting beneath the dignity of an earl. If that is the case, " the old player " or " retired player " would fit him exactly. In

January, 1595, Derby married Elizabeth de Vere, his marriage having been postponed for some months, so that we can well understand that old scandals would be most unwelcome during the last six months of 1594. In addition, if it were widely known that an earl had been publishing poetry, it would be worse than a scandal—it would be a disgrace to his great name and the dignity of the House of Derby. Furthermore if Derby were shown to be W. S. (" the old player "), the author of *Lucrece* and therefore Shakespeare, the whole dangerous secret of the authorship of the propaganda plays (*Richard II* and *III*) was in jeopardy. It is therefore not difficult to see why *Avisa* was suppressed and why the author had to throw out a smoke-screen and back-date the poem out of the danger zone.

Now, as part of this smoke-screen, Dorrell states that he found a note from Willobie saying that " I know one ' A. D.' that either hath or would, if occasion offered, indure these, and many greater temptations, with a constant mind and a settled heart." From this we may not unreasonably infer that Avisa's married surname began with a " D." Could it possibly be Davenant ? If so, the opportunity of picking up a lot of old scandal and making sense out of it, as Mr. Lucas has done, is too good to be missed.

Sir William Davenant, the poet, born in 1605, was apparently proud of, and encouraged, the tradition that he was Shakespeare's natural son. In the Hatfield MSS. there is a letter written in 1599 by the Countess of Southampton to her husband, who was then serving in Ireland with Essex. Lady Southampton's letter reads : " All the news that I can send you that I think will make you merry is that I read in a letter from London that Sir John Falstaff is, by his Mistress Dame Pintpot, made the father of a goodly miller's thumb, a boy that is all head and very little body ; but this is a secrit."

Now it is believed that Sir John Falstaff was used as a code-name for Shakespeare—but why on earth should Southampton

and Lady Southampton be so amused at Shakespeare's amours ?
And why this secrecy ? But if we assume that Dame Pintpot
was Mrs. Davenant, the first wife of John Davenant, who kept
the Crown at Oxford, where tradition says that Shakespeare was
a frequent visitor, then the odds and ends of this old scandal
begin to become intelligible. And if " Sir John Falstaff" and
the Earl of Derby were one and the same person, the need for
secrecy would be pressing. But there is no very obvious joke
unless Avisa, as Mrs. Davenant, is Dame Pintpot (of *Henry IV*)
and unless the H. W. of the poem is Henry Wriothesly, the Earl
of Southampton.

Avisa probably originated from near West Knoyle, where
Henry Willobie lived and later it seems possible that she was,
as Davenant's wife, at the Crown (or Golden Cross) at Oxford
and since Falstaff, in *Henry IV* (I), II, IV, calls Mrs. Quickly
" Good Pint-pot " also, at some time or other, Mistress of a
Tavern in Eastcheap whence it would seem that she moved (in
the *Merry Wives*) to The Garter, at Windsor.

For Southampton to learn that an old flame of his had finally
surrendered to the " old player," and presented him with a son
(whether true or not), might well have been considered an
excellent joke—more especially by Lady Southampton.[1] Sir
William Davenant, if indeed he was a natural son of Shakespeare,
for which there is no evidence, would then have been a younger
half-brother of the " Miller's Thumb."

(9) *Histriomastix* was first produced in 1599, but the author
is unknown. Some time before 1610 a few lines were interpolated obliquely referring to Shakespeare. Some believe the
interpolation was written by Marston, who deservedly had
the reputation of a gadfly and stung anyone if opportunity
offered.

---

[1] Lady Southampton (*née* Elizabeth Vernon) had been a maid of honour to Queen
Elizabeth. She had no great reputation for virtue and had been Southampton's mistress.
He married her when she was about to have a child, for which both were sent to prison.

Enter Troilus and Cressida

Tro. Come Cressida, my cresset light,
Thy face doeth shine both day and night,
Behond, Behold thy garter blue
(line missing here)
Thy Knight his Valiant elboe wears,
That When he Shakes his furious Speare
The foe in shivering fearfull sort
May lay him down in death to snort.

As everyone knows, *Troilus and Cressida* is the only play of Shakespeare which depends on the real infidelity of a wife. In the above lines there seems no doubt that W. Shake-Speare is here called a Troilus. But what is far more interesting is that Troilus says : " Behold thy garter blue," because it suggests that the author of these lines considered Shakespeare to have been a Knight of the Garter. Now we know that Derby was made a Knight of the Garter on April 6th, 1601, and we know also that Derby was at one time consumed with jealousy because he believed, probably wrongly, that his wife had been unfaithful to him. Oxford also was a Knight of the Garter, so was Rutland. All three, Derby, Oxford, Rutland, had married lives sufficiently unsatisfactory to expose them to Marston's jibes, which could fit any one of them. Bacon was, of course, not a Knight of the Garter, nor, most certainly, was the Stratford actor. If, then, the author of these lines knew what he was talking about, and they are quite pointless if he did not, then either Derby or Oxford or Rutland must be Shakespeare, for there is no one else to whom they could apply. Rutland, owing to the late date on which he was born, 1576, must in my opinion be eliminated—leaving Oxford and Derby. But Oxford died in 1604. Unfortunately, the exact date of the interpolation is not known, but obviously the lines are more likely to refer to Derby, who had so lately been made a Knight of the Garter, than to Oxford, who had been made a K.G. many years before.

(10) About 1611 John Davies of Hereford wrote the following epigram in the *Scourge of Folly* :

> To our English Terence, Mr. Will Shake-speare :
> Some say good *Will* (which I, in sport, do sing)
> Had'st thou not plaid some Kingly parts in sport,
> Thou had'st bin a companion for a *King* ;
> And beene a King among the meaner sort.
> Some others raile ; but, raile as they thinke fit,
> Thou hast no rayling, but a raigning Wit :
> *And* honesty *thou sow'st which they do reape ;*
> *So, to increase their* Stocke *which they do keepe.*

John Davies was best known as a writing-master. He was a poet and protégé of the Derby family, having been intimately acquainted with them over many years. He was in fact a tutor to members of Ferdinando's family and probably responsible for the beautiful handwriting (when he chose to write well) of the 6th Earl of Derby. Davies dedicated his *Summa Totalis* to Lord Ellesmere and " my good Lady and mistress, the Countess of Derby " in 1607. (This is Alice, the wife of the 5th Earl and the Amaryllis of Spenser's poem.)

It is interesting to observe how frequently allusions to Shakespeare come from protégés of the House of Derby. If there was a secret in the Derby family concerning the authorship of the plays of Shakespeare, then John Davies was certainly one of the few, outside a small aristocratic circle, who would have known it.

The first thing to note about this epigram is that it is addressed to an *amateur* actor. The line :

> " Hads't thou not plaid some Kingly parts in sport "

would have no meaning if addressed to a professional player. It is quite impossible to apply it to the Stratford actor.

The word *King* at the end of the fourth line was for some definite reason put into italics by the author—so that one might quite justifiably read " Queen " instead of " King," just as

" Prince " was quite commonly used by Elizabeth and others for " Queen." If these cryptic lines are taken as an allusion to Lord Derby, the 6th Earl, then the meaning, almost of every word, stands out clearly.

We know that the Catholics considered William to be the most suitable successor, preferable even to his elder brother Ferdinando,[1] who had somewhat degraded himself by marrying the daughter of a mere knight. There is evidence in a letter (1595) to Sir Robert Cecil (Titherley) that William Stanley was a keen amateur actor. With these possibilities in mind the general interpretation of the Epigram becomes clear, thus :

Some say (good Will) if you had not degraded yourself by sportingly acting the part of a King you might have been the Queen's consort and have succeeded to the throne as a King " among the meaner sort."

Mr. R. M. Lucas, from whose book, *Shakespeare's Vital Secret,* I have taken the above interpretation, suggested that the " meaner sort " means that his descent was through the female line, and this has been confirmed through parallel uses of the phrase cited by Titherley.[2]

The first line of Davies's epigram is interesting. For many reasons one would have expected that Shakespeare would have been compared to Plautus rather than to Terence. But it may be that Terence was chosen, as Sir George Greenwood suggested, because he is " the one Latin author whose name is alleged to have been used as a mask name or *nom de plume* for the writings of great men, who wished to keep the fact of their authorship concealed."

Furthermore, we note that the hyphenated name Shake-Speare is used. By this hyphen Davies makes it clear that he is not referring to Shakspere the actor, who anyway pronounced his name Shaxpur and whose name was *never* hyphenated.

---

[1] *A conference on the Succession* by Doleman, alias Parsons, (See Allusion 11.)
[2] Eg., Part I, *Henry VI.* (11. 5, 122)

(11) John Speed,[1] in his *History of Great Britain,* published
in 1611, makes a strong protest (Book IX, Ch. 15, para. 47)
against someone (who can only be Shakespeare) for making
Oldcastle a Ruffian, a Robber and a Rebel. Speed was an
ardent Protestant and Sir John Oldcastle the 1st Lord Cobham
was a Protestant " martyr " who was hanged in 1471. As is
well known, Sir John Oldcastle was the original name of Falstaff
and Shakespeare mocked and made a butt of him in *Henry IV,*
Pt. I and II, at first under the name Oldcastle. The 8th Lord
Cobham seems to have protested against this to Shakespeare,
who made amends by changing the name to Falstaff, and the
whole of the first edition of *Henry IV* was destroyed. In a
later edition, however, " Old " appears by an oversight instead
of " Fal " in a marginal stage direction. Furthermore, Prince
Hal addresses Falstaff as " My old lad of the castle " . .
(*Henry IV*, Pt. I, Act I, Scene 2). Shakespeare made further
amends by stating in the Epilogue of *Henry IV,* Pt. II, that
" Oldcastle died a martyr." All this is simple fact, but surely
it is extraordinary that, if the actor was the author, he was not
severely punished for his impudent mockery of Lord Cobham's
ancestor.

Now, one would expect that a straightforward historian like
Speed would have made his indignant protest about Shakespeare's
treatment of the martyr, Sir John Oldcastle, in a clear and
intelligible manner. But no ; as soon as the author of the
Shakespeare plays is referred to personally, everything has to be
wrapped in mystery. This is what Speed says. He protests . . .

" That N. D. author of three conversions hath made Ould-
castle a Ruffian, a Robber, and a Rebell, and his authoritie
taken from the Stage-players, is more befitting the pen of his
slanderous report than the credit of the judicious, being onely
grounded from this Papist and his Poet, of like conscience for

---

[1] R. M. Lucas first called attention to this important allusion in *Shakespeare's Vital
Secret.*

lies, the one ever faining, and the other ever falsifying the truth . . ."

N. D., without any doubt, stands for Nicholas Doleman—an alias of Robert Parsons, the notorious Jesuit agent, who was workng throughout Elizabeth's reign first for her overthrow, and later to establish a suitable pro-Catholic successor to the throne. As Nicholas Doleman he also wrote *A Conference on the Succession*, of which Shakespeare made not a little use in his plays. It was a most dangerous book to possess—loathed by Elizabeth and burnt by the common hangman, so that one wonders how the Stratford actor could possibly have had access to such a book. In this exceedingly rare book, after much discussion, William Stanley is preferred above all other pretenders as the Catholics' choice to succeed Elizabeth, as was first pointed out by Lucas.

Since the " Papist " (N. D.) referred to by Speed is certainly Parsons, there can be no reasonable doubt that the words of Speed, " Papist and his Poet," must mean Doleman (Parsons) and Lord Derby. Moreover, it follows that Speed knew Derby to be the author of *Henry IV* and responsible for mocking Sir John Oldcastle and creating Falstaff. No other explanation is possible.

(12) In 1599, William Jaggard published *The Passionate Pilgrim* by W. Shakespeare, but of the twenty pieces in this book only twelve were by Shakespeare. Thirteen years later a second and third edition was issued in which two poems by Thomas Heywood were included. Heywood was poet and dramatist, with a very considerable contemporary reputation. He was supposed to have written some two hundred and twenty plays, of which but few have survived. One of them, *A Woman killed with Kindness*, reaches a high level. Heywood's patron was the Earl of Southampton, but he was also a protégé of Lord Derby, whose playing company performed some of Heywood's plays.

When Heywood found that two of his poems were appearing in a book with Shakespeare's name on the title page, he promptly protested against the piracy to Nicholas Okes, his own publisher. We may note the extraordinary fact that Shakespeare had taken absolutely no notice of the impudent way in which Jaggard was using his name.

Jaggard then removed Shakespeare's name as author from the next edition of *The Passionate Pilgrim,* but thereafter continued to publish as before the protest. Heywood's protest in his *Apology for Actors,* 1612, was as follows :

" I must acknowledge my lines not worthy of his patronage under whom he hath publisht them, so the author I know [is] much offended with M. Jaggard that (although unknown to him) presumed to make so bold with his name."

As Thomas Heywood had a very high contemporary reputation, it is utterly unbelievable that he should say " acknowledge my lines not worthy of his patronage " as meaning the patronage of the Stratford actor. The lowly social position of an actor in those days is enough in itself to disprove it. No, without doubt Heywood considered that Shakespeare was in a social position much higher than himself—though it does not necessarily mean that he acknowledged Shakespeare to be a greater poet.

It is also obvious that Heywood knew the real name of Shakespeare, since he says : "the author I know [is] much offended with M. Jaggard." [1] Also, he says that the author (Shakespeare) did not know M. Jaggard, who had " presumed to make so bold with his name."

The exact meaning of the lines is none too clear—but one thing is certain : if Shakspere the actor had been Shakespeare the author, he could not help knowing Jaggard and knowing that his name was being used by Jaggard. If, however, Shakespeare

[1] Obviously Heywood knew that Shakespeare was alive in 1612, eight years after Oxford's death.

was some great nobleman, it is quite understandable that he would not know Jaggard, and that such a minor matter as his *nom de plume* being on the title page of an insignificant pirated book of poetry might easily escape his notice. In any case, he dare not take action if he wished to preserve secrecy.

John Donne's Holy Sonnets

(13) About 1618 the celebrated poet John Donne, a protégé and friend of the Derby family, dedicated six " Holy Sonnets " to E. of D. in the following terms :

> See, Sir, how as the Sun's hot Masculine flame
> Begets strange creatures on Nile's dirty slime [1]
> In me, your fatherly yet lusty Rhyme
> (For, these songs are their fruits) have wrought the same ;
> But though the engendering force from whence they came
> Bee strong enough, and nature doe admit
> Seaven to be born at once, I send as yet
> But six ; they say the seaventh wave hath still some maine ;
> I choose your judgement, wich the same degree
> Doth with her sister, your invention, hold
> As fire these drossie Rymes to purifie
> Or an Elixir, to change them to gold.
> You are that Alchemist wich always had
> Wit, whose one spark could make good things of bad.

Stratfordians state that this sonnet was addressed to the old Earl of Dorset, who had been the doyen among the poets of his day. This view is quite impossible, because John Donne, whilst being capable of writing a humble dedication to an Earl in accordance with the custom of the day, was not the sort of man to pay tribute in such glowing terms to the work of a very inferior poet—who in any case died in 1608, nine or ten years

[1] This reference to the Nile must surely have been prompted by *Anthony and Cleopatra*, II, VII, 20. If so this poem must have been addressed to Shakespeare as E. of D. It should also be noted that Donne speaks in the present tense, praising a poet who is *still alive* two years after Shakspere's decease.

before this sonnet was composed. In one anthology E. of D. is said to be the Earl of Doncaster. An impossible solution—because, as Titherley pointed out, there never was such an Earl, though James Hay, who was not even a poet, was made Viscount Doncaster in 1618. In truth, the praise is so full of sincerity and meaning that, coming from Donne, there is no one but Shakespeare worthy to receive it, or whom it so exactly fits. The " engendering force " is a magnificent expression, and the last two lines :

> You are the Alchemist wich always had
> Wit, whose one spark could make good things of bad.

perfectly describe what Shakespeare had been doing all his poetic life.

Who, then, is E. of D. ? Who else can he be but the Earl of Derby ?

Sir Thomas Stanley's Epitaph

(14) There is in Tong Church, in Shropshire, not far from Shrewsbury, an epitaph which was seen by the distinguished antiquarian Sir William Dugdale some time prior to 1664. The epitaph is to Sir Thomas Stanley, who was an uncle of the 6th Earl of Derby. Sir Thomas was reported to be an excellent musician and died in 1600.

Dugdale reports that the epitaph was written by " Shakespeare," and the flowing style confirms this.

On the eastern side :

> Aske who lies here, but do not weepe :
> He is not dead, he doth but sleepe.
> This stony register is for his bones,
> His fame is more perpetual than these stones ;
> And his own Goodness with himself being gone,
> Shall live, when earthly monument is none.

On the west side :

> Nor monumental stone preserves our fame,
> Nor skye-aspiring pyramids our name,
> The memory of him for whom this stands
> Shall out-live marble, and defacers' hands.
> When all to Time's consumption shall be given,
> Stanley, for whom this stands, shall stand in heaven.

The last punning couplet on the name Stanley, and the "conceit" that Stanley's memory shall outlive marble (see (Sonnet LV) are particularly reminiscent of Shakespeare. This epitaph is but one more connecting thread between Shakespeare and Derby, who probably erected this fine monument.

(15) *The I.M.S. Ode in the* 1632 *Folio.* (*Second Folio.*)

The Second Folio was a reprint of the First Folio with but few corrections, and these of little value, but at the beginning of the volume there is a truly magnificent ode to Shakespeare above the letters I.M.S. The first four lines run :

> A mind reflecting ages past, whose clear
> And equal surface can make things appear
> Distant a thousand years, and represent
> Them in their lively colours just extent.

It consists of seventy-eight lines and it is not necessary to quote further. Dr. Ingleby, the well-known Shakespearean scholar, says of this ode : " This noble composition. . . . This magnificent tribute to Shakespeare's worth. . . . The majestic flow and smooth run of the verse."

Many suggestions have been made as to who I.M.S. could be, but no really satisfactory answer has been discovered. John Milton Senior, or student ; Jasper Mayne, student ; John Marston, student, have been suggested but need only be mentioned to be rejected. Some have thought Donne or Chapman might have written the ode and signed it " In memoriam scriptoris " ; to my mind an equally unsatisfactory solution. Dr. Ingleby considered that I.M.S. must have been "a friendly rival of Shakespeare, who bore him no envy" and noted that he must have had considerable influence to impose this long poem on the editors of the Second Folio.

I have very little doubt that R. M. Lucas was correct and that this ode was written by James, the eldest son of the 6th Earl of Derby. James, Lord Strange, would have been twenty-six years old in 1632. He would normally sign himself James, or leaving out the vowels, as a measure of secrecy, I.M.S.

In 1642 James, Lord Strange, became the 7th Earl of Derby. He was known as the Great Earl of Derby and was no doubt a very remarkable man. He fought for the King in the civil war and was beheaded by Cromwell. This ode to Shakespeare signed I.M.S., though it cannot be regarded as evidence, would give, if Lucas is right, strong support to the connection between the Derby family and the works of Shakespeare.[1]

(16) *The Phœnix and the Turtle.*

An extraordinary poem was published in 1601, by R. C. (Robert Chester), in a volume called *Love's Martyr.* Several poets contributed prefatory matter and the book was "consecrated to the love and merit of the true noble Knight Sir John Salisburie." All the persons concerned were more or less connected with the Derby family. In this book is included the mystical poem called *The Phœnix and the Turtle* of which the meaning has never been fully fathomed. This poem was signed William Shake-speare. Now Ursula, Lady Salisburie, the wife of Sir John, was the natural daughter of the 4th Earl of Derby (William's father). The 4th Earl had recognised Ursula as his daughter and had permitted her to use the name Stanley. Ursula

---

[1] Dr. Titherley, who proposed Ben Jonson as the author, calculates that this ode was written by a man of about 70 and could not therefore have been by James, Lord Derby's son. To meet Titherley's objection I suggest that James asked his father for assistance. Derby then revised the ode and made a fair copy. Derby was seventy-one in 1632. We have no collateral evidence that James was capable of writing such a magnificent composition.

Stanley was therefore the 6th Earl of Derby's half-sister. So William Shake-Speare is here found contributing in a book, intimately associated with the Derby family, a poem, on a mourning theme, which must have been unintelligible except to members of the House of Derby.

ALLUSIONS

ALLUSIONS IN CHAPTER

(1) " Poor poet-ape." Epigram.
(2) *Every Man out of his Humour.*
(3) *Polimantea.*
(4) *The Return from Parnassus.*
(5) John Davies in *Microcosmos.*
(6) Edmund Spenser. *The Tears of the Muses.*
(7) Spenser. Ætion.
(8) *Willobie His Avisa.*
(9) *Histriomastix* (Marston).
(10) John Davies. *Scourge of Folly.* " To our English Terence."
(11) John Speed and Sir John Oldcastle.
(12) Thomas Heywood in *The Passionate Pilgrim.*
(13) John Donne's sonnet to E of D.
(14) Sir Thomas Stanley's Epitaph.
(15) The I.M.S. Ode in Second Folio (1632).
(16) *The Phœnix and the Turtle*

CHAPTER VII

VARIOUS PLAYS AND POEMS

Hamlet

IN Nashe's preface to Robert Greene's *Menaphon*, which Malone dated as 1589, there is a passage evidently referring to *Hamlet*.

> . . . yet English Seneca reade by Candle-light yields many good sentences . . . and . . . will affoord you whole Hamlets, I should say handfuls of tragical speeches.

Obviously the Stratfordians cannot for a moment allow that this old *Hamlet* to have been written earlier than 1589 by Shakspere of Stratford for, in 1586, according to tradition, he had not yet left Stratford. Sir Sidney Lee suggested that this *Ur-Hamlet* (as it is called) was written by Thomas Kyd—though there is very little to support this view.

Now, not only did this old play have in it "handfuls of tragical speeches" but according to Nashe's preface to Sir Philip Sidney's *Astrophel and Stella* (published in 1591) it also apparently had in it a "to be or not to be" speech. This is not, however, a certainty. According to Lodge's *Wits Misery*, published in 1596, there seems also to have been a ghost in the play which cries out "Hamlet Revenge !"

In 1594, Henslowe notes in his diary that a play called *Hamlet* was acted by the Lord Chamberlain's men (Shakspere's company) at the Newington Butts theatre. Henslowe's entry is "9 of June 1594, R'd at hamlet VIII^s." It was Henslowe's custom to mark a first performance as n.e. (new enterlude). As he did not do so on this occasion we may conclude that *Hamlet* was an old play in 1594. In 1602, a book called the *Revenge of Hamlet, Prince of Denmark*, was entered at the Stationers' Company and in 1603 the first quarto, entitled *The Tragicall Historie of Hamlet Prince of Denmark*, by William Shakespeare, appeared. This is the first appearance of Shakespeare's *Hamlet* admitted by the Stratfordians,[1] though there is some very strong but disputed evidence to show that it was well known long before this. Moreover the title page of the 1603 quarto bears the words : " As it has been divers times acted by his Highnesse servants in the Cittie of London : as also in the two Universities of Cambridge and Oxford, and elsewhere."

In 1604 another edition was published, the second quarto, in which the 1603 play was greatly enlarged and improved. The second quarto is more or less the *Hamlet* as we know it. How much of the master's hand is in the 1603 quarto has been the subject of much controversy. Some experts say that Shakespeare's modification of the old play had not gone much beyond the second act. Lee thought " Shakespeare's tragedy owed much to the lost version of *Hamlet*." In fact the evidence seems to indicate that the 1603 edition is the old *Hamlet*, with some revision, for the general action of the play in the 1603 quarto is very similar to that in the 1604 quarto.

Now Mr. Looney, in *Shakespeare Identified*, has demonstrated, conclusively in my opinion, that the plot, the main characters and many of the incidents of *Hamlet* reflect some of Oxford's actual life experiences. In the first place it is hard to believe that Hamlet is not a self-revelation of the author himself. This is the opinion of even orthodox critics, though one can hardly imagine two characters more fundamentally different than those of the Prince of Denmark and the Stratford actor.

Oxford of course was not a prince of royal blood, but he was the senior peer of England. Hamlet's admiration for his

---

[1] See Greenwood, p. 501 *et seq.*, for detailed discussion of *Hamlet* in *The Shakespeare Problem Restated*.

father is the basic motive of the play and Oxford's father, who died in 1562 when Edward was twelve years old, was by reputation exactly the sort of father who would have had the unstinted admiration of a boy of twelve. Oxford's mother married again, Sir Charles Tyrrell, and seems to have passed completely out of her son's life. The exact date of Lady Oxford's second marriage is not known. When she died in 1568, at Hedingham, " it looks," says Mr. Looney, " as though Oxford's stepfather had established himself on the family estates and may have appeared to the youth as having doubly supplanted his father, first in his mother's affections and then in the hereditary domains." Here we have a situation resembling that which we find in *Hamlet*. Polonius has been recognised by many critics as Lord Burleigh. For just as Ophelia was Polonius' daughter, so Anne Cecil (whom Oxford married) was Burleigh's daughter. Burleigh's character has been pictured by Macaulay, who says that he was somewhat jocose. He had more shrewdness than generosity— gave neatly expressed reasons for exacting money and keeping it carefully both for the public advantage and his own. Bacon has recorded some of his sportive sayings.

When it is remembered that Oxford detested Burleigh then (allowing for this) Polonius would be a good, if unkind, portrait of him. Burleigh's foibles are exaggerated and his wisdom is minimised. Yet the advice of Polonius to Laertes remains for ever famous for its shrewdness. Advice very similar to this was actually given by Burleigh to his son Thomas Cecil on his departure for Paris, so that Thomas Cecil could well be the original of Laertes. Burleigh employed a most extensive spy system which he used not only against the Queen's enemies but also against numerous other people including his own son, and no doubt also against Oxford, his ward. The instructions, given by Polonius to Reynaldo, to spy on his son Laertes, are therefore extraordinarily apt and barbed. It is known that Thomas Cecil, who was an older man than Oxford, by no means always saw eye to eye with his father. He was a brave, open-hearted soldier and a friend of Oxford. But Burleigh was very dissatisfied with his son's life in Paris. Mr. Looney tells us that Burleigh wrote to his son's tutor, Windebank, to say that he " has a watchword sent him out of France that his son being there shall serve him to little purpose, for that he spends his time in idleness."

We do not know enough of Oxford's married life to be able to say with any certainty what were the causes of its lack of success. Probably Oxford was too temperamental, arrogant and hot-tempered to be a satisfactory husband. Anne being Burleigh's daughter and Oxford Burleigh's ward, it does seem possible that Burleigh made use of his daughter to spy on his son-in-law, or at least Oxford may have thought that his wife was being used in this way. Certainly the motive of much of Hamlet's cruelty to Ophelia was caused by just such a suspicion.

In 1569 Oxford made repeated requests to be allowed to travel, but permission was refused by the Queen, almost certainly on Burleigh's advice.

Claudius said to Hamlet, who also wanted to travel :

> For your intent
> In going back to school in Wittenburg
> It is most retrograde to our desire.

Oxford, in fact, ran away to the Continent in 1574 and was chased and brought back—no doubt in a fury.

Hamlet's attitude to religion which might be described as somewhat free-thinking Catholicism, agrees remarkably well with Oxford's, for Oxford turned Catholic in 1581, and his name is on the lists of those whom Philip of Spain's agents hoped would support a Catholic uprising ; but it is doubtful whether he was a practising Catholic, and he was certainly not an ardent one.

The living man from whom the character of Horatio may

well have been taken is Sir Horace de Vere, Oxford's cousin, one of the foremost soldiers of the day. He was a man for whom Oxford had an immense respect, for not only had Sir Horace made a great reputation in a profession, in which Oxford would have liked to have excelled, though denied the chance, but Sir Horace had all that stability of character and that evenness of temper, whether in success or in failure, which Oxford reputedly lacked.

Consider Hamlet's dying words to Horatio :

> O God!—Horatio, what a wounded name,
> Things standing thus unknown, shall live behind me.

How well might these words have been said by Oxford to his cousin, Sir Horace de Vere—for the name that Oxford has, in fact, left behind is by no means a pleasant or a blameless one.

In the 1604 quarto, Hamlet is told that the skull he holds belonged to Yorick, the King's jester, who had " lain in the earth three and twenty years." It is possible that the author is here referring to the jester, John Heywood, who was given the title of King's jester by Henry VIII and died about 1580, so that, in 1604, it was true that he had been buried for twenty-three years. As Oxford and Derby were brought up at Court, Heywood might well have borne either " on his back a thousand times."

The greater the detail in which the play and Oxford's life are compared, the closer becomes the resemblance between the two and, by cumulative evidence, the more probable it is that the play of *Hamlet* incorporates experiences of Oxford's life.

It is therefore quite possible that when William Stanley visited the Earl of Oxford, say in 1587, he found an old play of *Hamlet*, not so very dissimilar from the 1603 quarto of *Hamlet*, already written, if not by Oxford then by someone who had intimate knowledge of Oxford's life.

With this old play as the basis, I think that Oxford and Derby henceforth worked in collaboration. If so the grave-digging scene must have been originally written by Stanley, for he had brought back with him from Navarre the story of the death of Helen of Tournon, as told to him probably by Queen Marguerite. It does not follow that because many of the incidents in *Hamlet* reflect Oxford's life, that Oxford, even if he had been the original writer of the *Ur-Hamlet*, was the real author of the final version. But it does follow that whoever wrote *Hamlet* had intimate knowledge of Oxford's private life and was of sufficient social standing to dare to record these intimate episodes in a play. As we know, Derby was Oxford's kinsman and son-in-law.

The Merry Wives of Windsor, etc.

There is a tradition that Queen Elizabeth was so taken with Falstaff that she asked Shakespeare to write a play showing Falstaff in love. Shakespeare is supposed to have responded by writing *The Merry Wives of Windsor* in fourteen days. Whether this is true or not it is clear that a number of names, Falstaff, Shallow, Bardolph, Pistol and Mrs. Quickly have been lifted out of *Henry IV* and introduced into *The Merry Wives*. There is in fact some evidence to show that the pirated and garbled quarto (1602) of *The Merry Wives* was written at great speed.

There are two facts about this play which are particularly interesting for our investigation :

(1) The accusation by Justice Shallow against Falstaff.
(2) The Garter passage, which has been dragged in quite unnecessarily; at least it has nothing to do with the play. (Act V.)

We know, largely owing to the investigation of Mrs. Charlotte Stopes, that the traditional episode in Shakspere's life of his poaching deer from Sir Thomas Lucy is a myth because there was no park in the neighbourhood where deer could be poached It follows that Shallow's accusations against Falstaff has no connection with Shakspere of Stratford's past. Dr. Leslie Hotson, who discovered that in 1595 Shakspere had been involved with a man called Langley and two females in a conspiracy to murder a man called William Wayte, has tried to identify Shallow with one James Gardiner, the father-in-law of William Wayte.

This identification is in the highest degree far fetched and unsatisfactory. It is not necessary to examine it in detail since Professor Abel Lefranc found a complete solution which entirely meets the case. It is a fact that just prior to 1602 a Justice of the Peace named Stephen Proctor was bringing an action in the Star Chamber against the agents of Lord Derby for killing deer, causing riot, etc. In fact Proctor was making exactly the kind of accusations against Derby which Shallow makes against Falstaff. Moreover Proctor's name with a capital " P " was actually introduced in the text of the 1602 quarto, but was suppressed after the dispute had been settled.

On May 26th, 1601, Lord Derby was installed at Windsor as a Knight of the Garter. The allusions to the Garter ceremonies at the end of the play, otherwise inexplicable, become full of meaning if they were fresh from the mind of a man who had just been invested with the Order of the Garter. They would have been a natural and graceful compliment to the Queen.

The Merry Wives, after being reprinted in 1619, three years after Shakspere's death, next appears in the First Folio, having been much expanded and with very numerous emendations. If they were not in the original manuscript we may well ask who made these extensions and improvements. Were they made after Shakspere's death? The question is reasonable because, apart from *The Merry Wives of Windsor*, several other plays were revised apparently after Shakspere's death and of course long after the death of Oxford. These improvements and additions are gratefully accepted by all scholars as Shakespeare's handiwork.

Take *Othello*: this play was first printed in 1622, six years after Shakspere's death, but when it appeared in the First Folio, in 1623, it had received a further 160 new lines and numerous and important alterations.

Again: the Contention plays representing *Henry VI*, Parts II and III, were reissued in 1619, three years after Shakspere's death, but, in the Folio plays, Part II of *Henry VI* contains 1578 new lines and is much altered otherwise.

Richard III. A quarto edition, the 6th edition, of this play, was printed in 1622, yet in the First Folio we discover the addition of 193 new lines and nearly 2,000 minor but nevertheless important corrections and improvements. The commentators have no hesitation in accepting these additions and emendations as having been made by Shakespeare himself. This is the opinion of the Cambridge editors and no one has contested it. The question then arises as to whether these changes were in the original manuscript or were made subsequently, and, if so, who made them.

The Stratfordians, of course, say that they were made before the death of the actor in 1616. But is this really so and what evidence have they ? For we are faced with a very extraordinary fact. In the 1622 quarto of *Richard III* there were twelve printers' errors and these errors have been reproduced in the Folio. It is impossible to avoid the conclusions that whoever made these alterations made use of and wrote them into a copy of the 1622 quarto, because the Folio printers certainly used this quarto, as amended, but failed to correct the printer's errors. But when the 1622 quarto first appeared, Shakspere had been dead for six years ; also Oxford and Rutland were long since dead. Of the possible Shakespearean candidates, only Bacon and Derby survived. Reasons for disbelieving that Bacon wrote the plays of Shakespeare have already been given, whilst from 1623 onwards Derby lived in complete retirement, mainly at Chester, and I do not doubt that he continued to revise the plays at least up to that date.

After 1623 no further plays could have been published under the name of Shakespeare. Whether Derby wrote further plays, which never saw the light, after that date, is of course unknown. If he did they were lost, probably with the rest of the Derby MSS., when Lathom was destroyed in the civil war.

Othello

Mr. Looney, in *Shakespeare Identified*, attempted to show that *Othello* reflects some of the experiences of Oxford's life and employs the following arguments. It had been Oxford's intention to prolong his voyage abroad and to visit Cyprus, among other places. From the Hatfield manuscripts, Mr. Looney tells us that " certain facts specially relevant to our argument already stand out boldly and distinctly. The first is that he (Oxford) expresses a warm regard for his wife. The second is that a responsible servant of his, his receiver, had succeeded in insinuating into his mind suspicions of some kind respecting Lady Oxford. The third is that her father, for some reason or other, recalled Oxford to England, thus upsetting his project of extended travel. The fourth is that on his return he treated his wife in a way quite inexplicable to her, refusing to see her ; whilst she, for her part, showed an earnest desire to please him. The fifth is that reports unfavourable to Lady Oxford's reputation gained currency. And the sixth is that there seems to have been no shadow of justification for these reports."

Comparing these facts concerning Oxford's life with the play *Othello*, Mr. Looney continued :

" Brabantio, the father-in-law of Othello was, like Oxford's father-in-law (Burleigh), the chief minister of state. . . . Othello himself, like Oxford, was one who took his stand firmly

and somewhat ostentatiously upon the rights and privileges of
high birth. . . . Desdemona is represented as one who, in the
words of her father, ' was half the wooer,' just as Anne Cecil is
represented. . . .

"Iago, the arch-insinuator of suspicion, is Othello's own
' ancient,' and occupies a position analogous to Oxford's receiver,
who had dropped the poison of suspicion into his master's
mind." Both Oxford and Othello have the same grounds for
discontent—their recall home from abroad—for Desdemona
says :

> Why do you weep ?
> Am I the motive of these tears, my lord ?
> If haply you my father do suspect,
> An instrument of this your calling back,
> Lay not the blame on me.

This, as far as one can judge, is the pathetic and puzzled
attitude of Anne. Further, as Mr. Looney says: " It is worth
while remarking that Othello was called back from Cyprus :
the very part of the world that Oxford was prevented from
visiting by his recall ; and that he was called back to Venice,
the city which Oxford had just left." Oxford and Othello
have exactly the same cause for jealous rage—unjust suspicion of
their wives.

Mr. Looney has made out an interesting case for showing that
the author of Othello, as well as of Hamlet, had intimate knowledge of Oxford's life, but he is no nearer proving that *Othello*
was written by Oxford. *Othello* could have been written at
least equally well or better by his son-in-law Derby, who not
only knew all about his life, but was really acquainted with the
Mediterranean.

All's Well that Ends Well

Some researches of outstanding importance (page 116) have
recently been published by Professor G. Lambin in France.

Lambin has demonstrated that Shakespeare, whoever he was, had a remarkably intimate knowledge of Florence, Verona and Milan. Florence, of course, figures in *All's Well that Ends Well*, but it is not the main plot which is of special interest, because this was surely taken, with minor alterations, directly from Boccaccio. It is the many alterations and additions and the sub-plot which throw such a flood of light on Shakespeare's knowledge not only of Florence but of Paris and the detailed topography of France as well as of the complicated politics of the day. Professor Lambin has traced out and made sense of Helena's travels : he has shown that Chateau Roussillon was situated in the Rhone Valley south of Lyons, some twenty miles north of Tournon, and was the seat of the Counts of Roussillon. He proves that Helena, who takes the place of Gillette in Boccaccio's story, was a real person—the daughter of Claudine de la Tour, Baroness de Tournon and Dowager Countess of Roussillon, lady-in-waiting to Marguerite de Valois, the Queen of Navarre. So this is the same Helen of whose sad fate we hear in *Love's Labour's Lost*, Act V, 2, 11. The story of her death from unrequited love, brought to light by Professor Lefranc, is the source from which Ophelia's death in *Hamlet* was taken. Furthermore, Professor Lambin has shown that the author of *All's Well that Ends Well* has satirised in this play a number of the most notable and notorious but easily identifiable personages of the day, in a manner only possible for an author who had moved in the very highest circles of Italy and France.

Although Lambin's researches on this play are not decisive as between Oxford and Derby, they constitute a clear proof that Shakspere of Stratford, who never visited either France or Italy, could not possibly have written either *All's Well that Ends Well* or *Two Gentlemen of Verona*.

Moreover, Dr. Colafelice [1] of Verona has recently discovered

---

[1] A private communication from Dr. Titherley.

a letter to the Spanish governor of Milan from a spy referring to a visit to Verona of two " Cavaliers," H. S. and W. S., in July 1591, believed to be Southampton and Stanley. Details are at the moment (July 1954) not yet available. But the discovery may prove to be of great interest, since the date of this visit was the time (Titherley) when the first draft of *Romeo and Juliet* was written. Later, in June 1955 I visited Dr. Colafelice in Verona and he kindly told me of his researches. It seems that Shakespeare, arriving April 1591, stayed for at least two months in the house of Count Sarago. He has discovered a map of Verona by Jonnanes Nachius, dated 1615, which shows that Shakespeare had accurate knowledge of the streets and topography of Verona when writing *Romeo and Juliet*.

The Tempest

It is very remarkable that *The Tempest,* a play dealing with magic as the basis of the plot, should have been played before King James I. Professor Chambers gave the date as 1611, when it was first played before the Court.

James's abhorrence of all forms of magic and witchcraft is well known and the most severe laws were passed for the discovery and punishment of anyone suspected of practising these dangerous arts. Hatred of witchcraft became an obsession with James and those who mentioned magic in their writing treated it as an unmitigated evil. *The Tempest* was the exception, for in it we see that there can be good as well as bad magic. At all events the production of *The Tempest* at Court was an extremely bold act and one likely to incur the grave displeasure of the King. No one but an author of high rank, greatly respected by the King and of known loyalty, would have dared to preach, as Shakespeare does, a lesson of moderation so contrary to the King's policy and convictions in the matter of magic. In fact, only an aristocratic Shakespeare could have written

The Tempest, which is aristocratic in tone throughout, reflecting as it does the point of view of a great lord accustomed to handle men and give orders to his inferiors.

It is as impossible to conceive that Shakspere of Stratford wrote *The Tempest* as it is to imagine that he wrote *Love's Labour's Lost* when he first arrived in London, or the Great Tragedies when he was a prosperous but apparently bookless, landowner and money-lender at Stratford, occupied with numerous petty legal squabbles. Nor is it possible that Oxford had any hand in writing *The Tempest.*

NOTES TAKEN FROM PROFESSOR G. LAMBIN'S RESEARCHES
" SUR LA TRACE D'UN SHAKESPEARE INCONNU "
Published in Les Langues Modernes
1951 to 1953

Measure for Measure

No one knows the year in which *Measure for Measure* was originally composed. It was published for the first time in the 1623 Folio and there are reasons (Titherley) for believing that it was probably taken from a copy of a copy after having been revised several times.

The usual sources given are *Cinthios Hecatommithi* of 1565, translated into French in 1584, and *Promus and Cassandra,* by George Whetstone, published in 1578. But Shakespeare introduced numerous modifications and additions to these versions of the story ; besides new names and new characters. For instance, in the play the scene is Vienna instead of Innsbruck. Corvinus, King of Hungary, becomes Duke of Vienna, and remains incognito near his capital. Claudio's crime is much attenuated. Isabella is about to enter a convent of nuns of the " Clare "

Order. Angelo has a cast-off fiancée. Bernardin, Lucio and Escalus are new characters. But the real scene of Shakespeare's play is laid in Paris in 1582, and not Vienna, as we shall see.

Professor Lambin's discoveries are of outstanding interest to our quest, because William Stanley arrived in Paris on July 25th, 1582, with his tutor Richard Lloyd, as will be recalled. These two waited in Paris for their " permit to travel abroad." The permit having arrived on 12th September, Stanley and his tutor moved on (exact date not known) to the neighbourhood of Angers, whence Lloyd on October 6th wrote acknowledging the receipt of the permit.

Now Lambin has proved that Henri III left Paris, for a private journey in France, on August 11th, 1582. In his absence a certain Claude Tonart was condemned to death on September 8th, but rescued from execution on September 22nd. The King returned to Paris on October 7th.

If it can be shown that the living drama enacted in Paris between August 11th and October 7th and the personalities in Paris are identifiable with the plot and characters of the play, we shall have taken a very long step towards identifying Stanley, who was there at the critical time, as the only possible author of *Measure for Measure*. The closer the details are studied the more certain it becomes that the play could have only been written by an eyewitness of these events.

In the play we find that Isabella is about to enter a convent of the Order of Saint Clare and that Francesca is the Mother Superior who initiates her. Her instructions conform exactly to the actual rules of this Order.

> You must not speak with men
> But in the presence of the Prioress :
> Then if you speak you must not show your face,
> Or, if you show your face you must not speak.

There were no Clare nunneries in England at the end of the sixteenth century. There had been three, but all were dissolved in 1538. Once more we note the astonishing accuracy and detail of Shakespeare's information.

Even the names Francesca and Isabella were not chosen by Shakespeare by chance, since The Clares were of the order of Francescans and it was Isabella of France, sister of Saint-Louis, who founded, in 1256, the Clarissa nunnery which Isabella herself entered, died there, and was canonised later. In 1582 Longchamp had become one of interesting places to visit from Paris, but not always on religious grounds. The severe rules of the order at Longchamp had long previously been greatly relaxed and it seems that a village had grown round the nunnery where the attractions were far from innocent ; all resulting from a papal " Bull " of " Mitigation " (1263) which ameliorated the strict rules of the order. In the play, Lucio says, " Behold, behold, where Madam Mitigation comes! " when speaking of the prostitute, Mrs. Overdone ; and Isabella also wishes (I, ɪɪ, 45) that the rules were stricter. In 1583 Henri III installed the monkish order of Hieronimites in quarters near Longchamp, whose principal founders were Thomas de Siena and Pierre (Peter) de Pise—the names of the two monks in *Measure for Measure*. The Duke, as a Friar in the play, took the name of Lodowick, a most suitable name for a descendant of Saint-Louis. It was also the habit of Henri III to go frequently into " retreat " at Vincennes, presumably for prayer and meditation, but not everyone in Paris was convinced that his " retreats " were for religious purposes. In the play, Lucio, that incorrigible scandalmonger, hints this opinion to the Duke (disguised), much to the Duke's indignation (III, ɪɪ, 127). When reporting Henri's disappearance to Vincennes, Lord Cobham always, even after living three years in Paris, spelt it Vincent, so that the reason why Shakespeare called the Duke Vincentio is easily explained. It was also Henri III's habit from time to time to disguise himself and behave as a monk.

Lucio is a clever skit on a courtier of Henri III, called Saint-Luc

(Francois d'Espiney), who was compelled by the King (as was Lucio in the play) to marry a repulsive and vicious woman, Mille de B'. Saint-Luc appears to have been an incorrigible practical joker and dropper of bricks—in fact Lucio in the play is rather a portrait than a caricature.

We now come to some names introduced by the author into the play quite gratuitously, because they have nothing to do with the plot—Flavius, Valentinus, Roland, Crassus and Varrius. Professor Lambin has discovered without the least doubt the real names of these and demonstrated their standing in Paris in 1582–4. Surely only an eye-witness, a resident in Paris at the correct date, could have brought them so unnecessarily into his play. Two other names, however, are even more significant. First Bernadin Mendoza, lately the Italian ambassador to England, but now ambassador in Paris, was frequently referred to, by Walsingham, Stafford and Derby in their letters, as Bernardino. Mendoza had been nine years in England and boasted of his crimes there, but Henri turned a blind eye to his villainy, just as the Duke in the play postponed punishing the criminal Barnardine. As for the second, Ragasoni, the Papal legate, who had been a bitter enemy of Elizabeth, there can be little doubt that in the play the pirate Ragozine was called after him.

In the play the morals of Vienna were so bad (as they were in Paris in 1582), that the Duke deemed it necessary to revive some old rigorous laws against immorality. He leaves to Angelo this unpleasant task and departs dressed as a monk. Claudio is arrested for seducing Julietta and condemned to death though he pleads that they were really married and Julietta agrees that her union with Claudio was by consent. It is agreed by characters in the play that this judgment is cruel and unjust, but Angelo will not relent. When, however, Isabella pleads with Angelo for her brother's life, Angelo agrees to pardon Claudio if Isabella consents to sleep with him (Angelo). The disguised

Duke in the meantime makes private inquiries and concocts a highly complicated plan to save Claudio, confront Angelo with his villainy, and marry off everyone whether they like it or not—Lucio to a whore (i.e., Mille de B'.) and Angelo to his cast-off fiancée.

Now let us see what actually happened in Paris in 1582 as reported from two sources, viz., 1. The *Registre-Journal de l'Estoile*, for the reign of Henri III, of which the only publication was (in French) in 1621, five years after the Stratford actor's death and 2. *l'Histoire Universelle*, which de Thou published (in Latin) in 1733.

Soon after the departure (on August 11th, 1582) of the King from Paris, Claude Tonart seduced the daughter of Jean Bailly, President of the Council. As a result of the complaints of the girl's parents and as an example Tonart was arrested and thrown into the prison whose governor was the Prévôt. Hence, probably, the name " Provost " used by Shakespeare for the man who combined the offices of both chief of the police and gaoler : a combination of offices only known in France and the Netherlands. Claude Tonart, like Claudio, pleaded that he was really married to the girl, and that by mutual consent she was his wife, and she agreed not only that she was a willing party to the union but that the major responsibility was hers.

Nevertheless Tonart was condemned to death but was rescued amid scenes of great indignation at the injustice of the sentence. Shortly afterwards (October 7th) the King returned from his retreat—as Cobham writes, " the King has said openly that he has long lived in private sort." Claude Tonart was pardoned but La Roche-Flavin (Flavius in the play) seems to have been blamed for having had some responsibility for the condemnation of Tonart. Obviously Claude Tonart is the Claudio of the play, but Angelo appears to be a composite mixture of a number of unpleasant people in positions of importance in Paris at that time. Jean Poisle, for instance, a councillor of Paris, was denounced for many crimes by a colleague and everyone expected to see him hung, but as a result of the pleadings of his wife he got off with a very light sentence. Malevault who succeeded him was no better. Another original of Angelo was councillor Jérôme Angenoust, who had the appearance of a saint but was " un rigoriste," not unlike Angelo, in character.

When these events took place in Paris in 1582 William Shakspere was a boy of eighteen, just about to marry Anne Hathaway at Stratford. William Stanley, alone of all possible candidates, was in Paris, staying at the court of Henri III and, in view of Lambin's researches, it is quite impossible that *Measure for Measure* could have been written, owing to the wealth of accurate detail, by anyone but an eye-witness of these events in Paris on which the play was so manifestly constructed.

Two Gentlemen of Verona

Dr. Karl Elze and Sir Edward Sullivan, two well-known orthodox commentators, have already proved the possibility of a journey by water from Verona to Milan in the 16th century, but quite lately Professor Lambin has shown, in still greater detail, not only that the journey was possible but that probably it was in those days the normal and certainly the safest way of travelling between these two towns. In *Two Gentlemen of Verona* Shakespeare not only displays intimate knowledge of the water-ways of Northern Italy, but also his topographical familiarity with Milan, its neighbourhood, its boundaries and its gates down to the minutest details. He knew that about six miles to the north of Milan, on the road to Mantua, there were then woods which were infested by robbers—as is confirmed from other sources.[1] He knew also where the well of St. Gregory was situated (N.E. of Milan) and that it was suitable as a lonely meeting place. He knew how the frontier ran between Milan

[1] *The Journey of Fynes Moryson*, first published 1617.

and Mantua and the best place to cross it. In these notes
I have, with his permission, followed Professor Lambin's
essay " Sur la trace d'un Shakespeare inconnu " and gratefully
acknowledge my debt. Lately having had the opportunity of
visiting Milan I was able personally to confirm the accuracy of
his observations.

The first part of the journey of Valentine and Proteus from
Verona is down the River Adige for some fifty kilometres and
thence to the River Po by a small canal which joins the two
rivers. The expression " the tide is now " (II, III) cannot mean
the ocean tide up the stream, for tides on the Adriatic are
practically non-existent and in any case the young men wished
to travel down the stream, so that " the tide " means the flood
water from the hills which, coming down through Verona,
would assist their voyage. Possibly such flood water was
needed to make the small inter-connecting canal between the
Po and the Adige navigable. Once on the Po there is no
difficulty in reaching Milan by ship, via the Naviglio Grande.
In Milan, the Duke resided in Castello Sforzesco. The inner
courtyard of this castle, known as the Rochetta, contained the
living quarters, the outside buildings being used for the soldiers'
barracks. Above the Rochetta there is a high tower, reached
from the living quarters and overlooking the outside courtyard.
It was surely in this tower that Silvia was locked up by her
justly incensed parent. There is a room at the very top of the
tower but otherwise there are no windows, so that Valentine's
planned attempt to rescue Silvia by rope ladder would have
been extremely hazardous. However, Shakespeare wisely pre-
vents the attempt from being actually made, for Valentine's
scheme is betrayed to the Duke by Proteus and Valentine is
exiled and escaped towards Mantua. He knows that the easiest
way to cross the Mantuan-Milan frontier is by leaving from the
" North Gate " or Como Gate and, after passing through the
woods around Monza, crossing the boundary bridge over the

River Adda at Trezzo. The distance of these woods from the town is given later by Sir Eglamour as three leagues—quite correctly. Silvia now makes her own plans to escape and follow Valentine. She talks to Eglamour, who, as he crosses the outer courtyard would be visible from her window in the tower, and arranges to meet him at Father Patrick's cell. Lambin has discovered that a certain Father Patrick Hely, a well-known Irish Franciscan Friar of those days was apparently passing through Milan at the time of the action of the play—1576. As a Francescan, he would naturally have had his cell in the beautiful Cistercian Abbey of St. Ambroglio, about half a mile from the castle. Silvia deceitfully gets leave from the Duke to go to confession at St. Patrick's cell and there, by appointment, meets Sir Eglamour. She is in a nervous state (very naturally) and fancies she is being followed—" go on, good Eglamour, out at the postern gate by the Abbey wall " she says. Now about a hundred yards from the Abbey wall there still remain (as I saw myself) two fine arches of the old city wall. These arches now are no longer used for traffic, but they are still known by the local inhabitants as " pusterla " the " postern." This was obviously the safest exit for Silvia and her escort. To go back through the city and out at the " North Gate " would have been a grave risk if she was being followed. The Duke, accompanied by Proteus and Julia, gives chase and makes for the " rising of the mountain foot that leads towards Mantua." This mountain foot is roughly three leagues from the city and on the road to Mantua. The wood where the *dénoument* takes place is thought by some commentators to be near Mantua ; but this is certainly wrong because Father Laurence, who has gone for a long walk in penance, sees Silvia in the forest and reports her flight to the Duke. This forest is therefore within walking distance of Milan and on the road towards the Milan-Mantuan frontier.

These are only scanty notes of Lambin's detailed exposition but are enough to prove that Shakespeare could not have written this play unless he had had intimate first-hand knowledge of Milan and its neighbourhood.

Venus and Adonis and *Lucrece*

These two long poems are of such importance in our Quest for Truth that a few further notes entailing some repetition are desirable. *Venus and Adonis* is of very special interest if only because the author, for the first time, signed himself William Shakespeare ; that is in 1593, though it was certainly written a good deal earlier. Very naturally most Stratfordians date its composition to the months immediately before its publication, but other Stratfordians, including Sir Sidney Lee and Professor Churton Collins, believed that it must have been written several years earlier, because the poet called it " the first heir of my invention," when all scholars know that several Shakespeare plays were written before 1593. The latest Stratfordian authorities have now however realised that such an early date (say 1591 or earlier) for the composition of *Venus* would be extremely dangerous to the whole orthodox theory of author-ship. Even 1593 is embarrassingly early as it gives too little time for an unlearned Shakspere, but lately up from Stratford, to acquire enough culture not to say erudition to compose such a poem. The poet's definite but inconvenient statement that this poem is " the first heir of my invention " has been calmly disregarded by most Stratfordian scholars.

It is of interest that Dr. Titherley, by his new method of dating the works of Shakespeare, calculates that *Venus and Adonis* was written about 1585 when William Stanley was on his travels in the eastern Mediterranean where the myths of Venus and Adonis originated—thus conforming with the poet's admission that the poem was his first serious composition.

Apart from the dedication, there is no evidence that *Venus and Adonis* was in any way composed for the Earl of Southampton, but the dedication itself was probably written when the poem was revised, that is, shortly before publication. At that date Stanley was only the second son of an Earl, with little, if any, expectation of ever becoming Earl of Derby, and was then definitely of a lower social rank than Southampton. This fact fits very appropriately with the respectful tone of the dedication which reads :

To the Right Honourable Henry Wriothesly,
Earl of Southampton and Baron of Tichfield

Right Honourable,

I know not how I shall offend in dedicating my unpolished lines to your lordship, nor how the world will censure me for choosing so strong a prop to support so weak a burden : only, if your honour seem but pleased, I account myself highly praised, and vow to take advantage of all idle hours till I have honoured you with some graver labour. But if the first heir of my invention prove deformed, I shall be sorry that it had so noble a god-father, and never after ear so barren a land, for fear it yield me so bad a harvest. I leave it to your honourable survey, and your honour to your heart's content : which I wish may always answer your own wish and the world's hopeful expectation.

Your honours in all duty,

William Shakespeare.

When however, a year later (May 1594), the dedication to *Lucrece* was written, also to Southampton, Stanley's father, the 4th Earl and Stanley's brother, the 5th Earl, were both dead and Stanley had just become the 6th Earl of Derby. The tone of the dedication to *Lucrece* is accordingly entirely different, for it is now couched in normal terms of friendship between men of equal rank, such as would be written by one Earl to another. It reads :

TO THE RIGHT HONOURABLE HENRY WRIOTHESLY
EARL OF SOUTHAMPTON AND BARON OF TICHFIELD

The love I dedicate to your lordship is without end : whereof this pamphlet without beginning, is but a superfluous moiety. The warrant I have of your disposition, not the worth of my untutored lines, makes it assured of acceptance. What I have done is yours : what I have to do is yours, being part in all I have, devoted yours. Were my worth greater, my duty would show greater : meantime, as it is, it is bound to your lordship, to whom I wish long life, still lengthened with happiness.

Your Lordships in all duty,

William Shakespeare.

Comparing these dignified and aristocratic dedications with the many sycophantic dedications of the period, the impossibility of their being addressed by an actor to a great Earl is more than ever obvious and it is truly astonishing that the Stratfordians have induced any rational critic to swallow such a fantastic improbability.

There is a further very important point with regard to the publication of these two poems. Of all the works of Shakespeare *Venus* and *Lucrece* alone were " seen through the press " by the author himself. Both poems were admirably edited with hardly a misprint or a typographical fault, and were brought out in *de luxe* editions. It cannot be proved, though many attempts have been made to do so, that after 1594, Shakespeare took the least interest in the publication of any of his works, and we may well ask why Shakespeare, who took such meticulous care with these two poems, thereafter took no steps to see that his compositions were correctly edited. Nor indeed did he make any effort to prevent piratical issues of his works or protest when plays by others were fraudulently published under his name or initials. No explanation has ever been given by Stratfordians, to cover these extraordinary facts.

But as Dr. Titherley first pointed out, when we remember that Stanley became the 6th Earl of Derby in 1594 then the reason why he thereafter ceased to publish anything more is evident. William Stanley as the son or brother of an Earl might, under the cover of a *nom de plume,* interest himself in such literary matters without much risk of compromising the great name of Derby, but as Earl of Derby he dared take so such risks, particularly in the latter part of the year 1594 and subsequently when a new danger arose. There are strong reasons for believing (p. 60) that soon after Derby became Earl the Queen envisaged him for state reasons as a possible consort; indeed right up to the time of her death there was at least a chance that he might be called on to succeed her. In 1594 and in the following years there were several subversive Catholic plots, and it was well known to Elizabeth and her advisers that Derby was looked on by the Catholics as a suitable successor.[1] Under such circumstances it is no wonder that Derby, jealously watched by the Queen, took extreme care to preserve the secret of authorship on the preservation of which, as Lucas first pointed out, it is possible that his life depended.

[1] *A Conference on the Succession,* by N. D. (Nicholas Doleman) (p. 97).

CHAPTER VIII

FIRST FOLIO AND BEN JONSON

THE common belief that Shakspere of Stratford wrote the plays and poems of Shakespeare has the nature of a religion, supported far more by tradition and faith than by reason or logic. As in most religions faith is strengthened rather than weakened by the necessity for believing in miracles. Nor is the Stratfordian religion without its prophet; but Ben Jonson, like some other prophets, whilst sometimes comforting the hearts of true believers with unforgettable words at other times delivered himself of ambiguous and contradictory sayings which have given good cause for dismay to the faithful.

Faith in the favourable testimony of "Honest Ben" is the keystone of the temple of orthodoxy and if this faith were to crumble or Ben's word were to be seriously doubted, then the whole edifice of the Stratfordian case, undermined by pregnant negatives and resting otherwise largely on literary miracles, would collapse and "leave not a rack behind."

We must therefore consider whether there are any reasons why Ben Jonson's word should be doubted; whether there is anything suspicious surrounding the publication of the First Folio of 1623; whether there is any reason to think that a great literary deception was practised by Jonson and others which became the foundation for the orthodox belief that the Stratford actor wrote the works of Shakespeare. Let us then consider the whole story of the First Folio, the sayings and writings of Jonson, Heminge and Condell, the portrait, the Stratford busts, to see whether there is a prima facie case for believing there is something queer, something abnormal to rouse our suspicions, about the whole affair.

In the first place, who decided, seven years after Shakspere's death, to issue a collective edition of all the plays? It could hardly have been Jonson, for up to that time the only notice Jonson had taken of Shakspere was to write the insulting " poet-ape " epigram, to introduce him as Sogliardo into a play and to remark to Drummond as late as 1619 that " Shakspeer wanted arte."

Who or what converted Jonson from contempt for the actor to admiration of the poet in 1623? Secondly, who guaranteed the First Folio financially? We are told it was issued at a price of £1—about £10 of our money—and it was most unlikely to be a financial success. Neither Jonson, Jaggard, Blount nor Heminge and Condell would have provided such a guarantee. Probably the " Incomparable Paire," the Earls Pembroke and Montgomery, to whom the First Folio was dedicated, financed the issue.

Now let us examine the Preface to the great Variety of Readers. It is signed by Heminge and Condell, two of Shakspere's fellow-actors, though Steevens and Malone[1] demonstrated long ago that beyond reasonable doubt, most, if not all of it, was written by Ben Jonson. The opening paragraph is pure Jonsonese and it is extremely improbable that the two actors Heminge and Condell could have been capable of such a composition. Even Lee suggests " that they delegated much of their editorial duty to the publisher, Edward Blount, who was not unversed in the dedicatory art." [2]

The contents of this quaint address are of highest importance. After stating that they were friends of the author who was dead, Heminge and Condell continue with these remarkable words— " as where (before) you were abus'd with diverse stolne, and

[1] Malone. *Shakespeare*, Vol. 11, p. 663.
[2] See Sir Sidney Lee's *William Shakespeare*, p. 558-9.

surreptitious copies, maimed, and deformed by the frauds and stealthes of injurious imposters, that expos'd them : even those are now offer'd to your view cur'd, and perfect of their limbes ; and all the rest absolute in their numbers, as he conceived them. Who, as he was a happie imitator of Nature, was a most gentle expresser of it. His hand and mind went together. And what he thought, he uttered with that easinesse, that wee have scarse received from him a blot on his papers."

Now this can only mean that Heminge and Condell had received from the author his own autograph MSS. of the plays just as he wrote them down and that Shakspere wrote so fluently that there was hardly a blot (erasure) on the papers.

A more absurd statement has never been made. Who could possibly write *Hamlet* or *Lear* without " blots " and alterations ? We know in fact that Shakespeare repeatedly revised his plays. We might suppose that the editors received fair copies—in which case their remarks would have no point—but it is quite certain that they did not receive even fair copies of many of the plays, and freely utilised the available quartos.

As a result of much time and scholarship the sources from which much of the First Folio was derived are fairly well known. As Lee says : " But external and internal evidence renders it highly improbable that Shakespeare's autographs were at the printer's disposal. Well nigh all the plays of the First Folio bear internal marks of transcription and revision by the theatrical managers. In spite of their heated disclaimer the editors (Heminge and Condell) sought help too from the published quartos. But most of the pieces were printed from hitherto unprinted copies which had been used for theatrical purposes."

We have therefore to decide whether Heminge and Condell made these extremely important but false statements (with others equally untrue) quite deliberately or whether, as is far more probable, they signed on the dotted line probably for a suitable sum of money. This latter suggestion, so distasteful to modern Stratfordians, is supported by Messrs. Clark and Glover, the editors of the *Cambridge Shakespeare* (1865), who thought it possible that "The Preface may have been written by some literary man in the employment of the publishers, and merely signed by the two players."

We will adopt this view as being the more reasonable solution of the two—in which case we must lay the grave inaccuracies in the Preface to Jonson's account. The players' Dedication is even more Jonsonian than the Preface, for passages in it were clearly taken, as Sir George Greenwood pointed out, from Pliny and Horace.

So Heminge and Condell, the nominal editors, having been proved unreliable witnesses, no weight can be given to their testimony. But why did Jonson, or whoever was responsible for the production of the First Folio, select a couple of common actors to edit it? Since books were first printed there can surely never have been a more difficult editorial task, nor one more inefficiently accomplished; for the text of the First Folio is filled with errors of every description.

The probable answer is that if by design the plays were to be fathered on Shakspere of Stratford the most convincing proof would be a statement of two of Shakspere's fellow-actors saying that they knew Shakspere had written the plays. The two actors selected were those who had received legacies in his will and, Burbage being dead, these two had presumably been Shakspere's best friends.

But are there any other facts to arouse suspicion about the production of the First Folio, besides the fact that Heminge and Condell made grossly inaccurate statements both in their Preface and also in their Dedication to the "Incomparable Paire"? There most certainly are.

Take first the Droeshout engraving which appears on the title page. If there was nothing else to be suspicious about in the First Folio the Droeshout engraving alone is quite sufficient to arouse at any rate dismay and curiosity. Gainsborough, writing in 1768, said of it : " Damn the original picture of him . . . for I think a stupider face I never saw except D . . . K.'s— it is impossible that such a mind and ray of heaven should shine with such a face and pair of eyes."

How could the editors have selected such a frightful picture ? Is it a jest of sorts ? Must we really try to believe that our Shakespeare looked like this ? The head is too large for the body—the oafish eyes, the bulging hydrocephalic forehead, the stubbly moustache and the poorly shaved face all combine to give a revolting picture. But if we examine it more closely we can see that the face is not a portrait of a living man, but a mask. From the left ear to the chin there is a well-defined line marking the edge of the mask. When we look at the clothes, in which this effigy is dressed, there is no longer any doubt that we are confronted with some sort of fake, for there are two left arms as any competent tailor will confirm. " Let not thy right hand know what thy left hand doeth " is a quotation as well known to the Elizabethans as to us.

There is some substance in the suggestion that the editors at first intended to include quite a different picture. Of the two hundred or so copies of the First Folio now existing, Sir Sidney Lee informs us that " of these fewer than twenty are in a perfect state, that is with portrait printed (not inlaid) on the title page." In the copy in the library of Trinity College, Dublin, for instance, Judge Webb tells us that " the flyleaf is pasted on the title page." Martin Droeshout, the designer of this engraving, was only fifteen years old when Shakspere died, so that it is improbable that he ever saw the Stratford actor and yet we are assured that this is the only authentic portrait. For many reasons we must reject this as a portrait of Shakespeare and also it seems we must accept the fact that we have no portrait even of Shakspere—for every supposed portrait, the Chandos,[1] the Felton, the Hansen, the Lomley, the Stratford, are all without exception fakes or forgeries ; apart from the fact that they all differ from each other. Ben Jonson was no fool—he was moreover a shrewd judge of a picture—and it is impossible to believe that he thought this grotesque engraving with its mask-like face and two left arms was a genuine likeness to " The Soul of the Age " or even of the Stratford actor.

On the title page under the engraving Ben wrote the well-known lines :

> This Figure that thou here seest put,
> It was for gentle Shakespeare cut ;
> Wherein the Graver had a strife
> With Nature, to out-doo the life :
> O, could he but have drawne his wit
> As well in brasse, as he hath hit
> His face ; the Print would then surpasse
> All, that was ever writ in brasse.
> But, since he cannot, Reader, looke
> Not on his Picture, but his Booke.
>
> B. I.

The exact meaning of the first eight lines, even to an un-suspicious mind, is far from clear, but there can be no doubt about the excellent advice given in the last two.

It is not necessary to discuss here all the many possible meanings which can be read into these lines. I merely wish to point out that the engraving above them, together with the ambiguity of the lines, gives us good reason for believing that Jonson knew perfectly well that this was not a portrait of Shakespeare.

Now let us turn to the busts of Shakespeare. There is only one, the uninspiring effigy of a particularly stupid-looking man within the monument at Stratford, which has any pretences to authenticity. Some monument must have been erected before 1623, but except that the present bust has a bald head and thick

---

[1] Dr. Titherley considers that the Chandos portrait is one of Shakspere of Stratford. It is the picture of a swarthy man with rather a sly face and rings in the ears.

hair above the ears it has no resemblance whatever to the
Droeshout engraving. The only two authentic likenesses have
no resemblance to each other !

Now early in this century the diligent Mrs. Charlotte Stopes[1]
made the surprising discovery that the present Stratford bust is
not the original bust at all. For Sir William Dugdale, the author
of *History of the Antiquities of Warwickshire*, who visited Stratford
about 1636, introduced into his great work an engraving of
the original Stratford monument. It is sufficient to say that,
except for the bald head and the thick hair, the Dugdale engraving
in no way resembles either the Droeshout engraving or the
present bust. The Dugdale engraving depicts a melancholy man
with a drooping moustache and with his hands on a sack of
wool or malt, not on a cushion as now. It may of course be a
mere coincidence, but this melancholy man's face bears quite a
distinct resemblance to the picture of Bacon in *Sylva Sylvarum*.
No one knows who erected the original bust or who took
it down, probably in 1749, and erected the present one, but
it is reasonable to suppose that whoever was responsible for
the First Folio was also responsible for the erection of the
original bust.

Below both the present (and the original) bust are two Latin
lines, which translated mean :

" In judgment a Nestor, in genius a Socrates, in art a Virgil.
The earth covers him, the people mourn for him, Olympus
has him."

Apart from Shakespeare there was only one man in all England
in 1623 to whom these attributes could justly apply. Nestor
is typical of the elder statesman, who gives sage advice. Socrates
was the originator of a new philosophy and Virgil is the artist
in words. They could apply to Bacon, but the succeeding lines
show that they were to " Shakespeare." Were they part of the
general deception ?

[1] Mrs. C. Stopes in *Monthly Review*, 1904.

Now let us turn to the magnificent ode which Jonson wrote in the First Folio in honour of Shakespeare. It contains some very remarkable, significant and famous lines, but it is so well known that it is not necessary to quote it. It is in praise of Shakespeare as a poet, but with the exception of four words there is nothing in it from beginning to end that indicates, in any way, who the man Shakespeare was. It might equally well have been in praise of Shakspere of Stratford, or of Oxford, or of Derby, or of Bacon or of any other candidate. These four words which apparently connect the works of Shakespeare with the Stratford actor are : " Sweet Swan of Avon."

If another significance can be given to these words then the only connections between the First Folio and Shakspere of Stratford are the Dedication and the Preface signed by Heminge and Condell and the short poems by very minor poets who perhaps really thought Shakespeare was Shakspere. But we have seen these two Players are strongly suspect as witnesses and the opinion of the minor poets is of small consequence.

Let us take the four significant words in their context :

> *Sweet Swan of Avon !*   What a sight it were
> To see thee in our waters yet appeare,
> And make those flights upon the bankes of Thames,
> That so did take Eliza, and our James.

It will be noted that this apostrophe is to the Poet himself and might well be addressed to a living man. Shakespeare's plays were, at the time, being produced repeatedly in London so that Jonson cannot be suggesting that the plays should be seen in London. No, surely he is hoping that the Poet himself will visit the banks of the Thames.

There are six Avons in England and though it is possible that Jonson used the expression " Sweet Swan of Avon " ambiguously just because it could be taken to refer also to the Stratford Avon, nevertheless it is the Wiltshire Avon which would be most naturally in his mind when he spoke of the River Avon. The

Wiltshire Avon though not large is a main river, while the Stratford Avon is a tributary of the Severn. For many years Jonson was employed by the Earl of Pembroke in repairing or decorating Wilton House near the Avon, three miles from Salisbury. It was to Wilton House that the Company to which Shakspere belonged was summoned in August 1603 and it was there that on occasion other plays of Shakespeare seem to have been performed. James I saw *As You Like It* performed there in October 1603, and stayed with his Court at Wilton for a couple of months when the plague was bad in London. Daniel, who spent much of his life at Wilton and was a tutor to William later Earl of Pembroke, wrote :

> Avon rich in fame though poore in waters
> Shall have my song, where Delia hath her seate.

Daniel here without doubt referred to the Wiltshire Avon, and when he died there an unknown poet wrote an epitaph calling Daniel " Sweetest Swan of Avon."

To James and his courtiers the River Avon would unquestionably have meant the Wiltshire Avon. Neither Elizabeth nor James, as far as we know, ever visited Stratford. Furthermore, the Earl of Pembroke, one of the " Incomparable Paire " to whom this Folio was dedicated, had his seat at Wilton House and for him the Avon would certainly mean the Wiltshire Avon.

If therefore there are other reasons for believing that Jonson was perpetrating a literary deception then the use of the expression " Sweet Swan of Avon " may well have been intended to serve a double purpose. It could induce ordinary people, when taken in conjunction with Heminge's and Condell's testimony and the minor poems, to think he was referring to Shakspere of Stratford, while at the same time enabling him to give praise, with a clearer conscience, to some other poet, whom he knew to be Shakespeare.

We will not here enter into a detailed discussion of other ambiguous passages in Jonson's superb ode to Shakespeare. Once the possibility is admitted that Jonson may have been writing double meanings into his lines there is no longer any difficulty in finding meanings satisfactory to all parties in this controversy. For instance, the famous line " And though thou hadst small Latin and less Greek " can quite grammatically be interpreted to mean " even had it been true that thou hadst small Latin and less Greek." Also regarding the verses under Droeshout's engraving it has been suggested that the lines :

> This Figure, that thou here seest put,
> It was for gentle Shakespeare cut ;

would have a totally different meaning if " for " in the second line was taken as meaning " instead of "—as it does in the line of Jonson's ode :

> Or *for* the lawrell, he may gaine a scorne.

In 1621 Bacon, then Viscount St. Alban, fell from power and into disgrace. He was accused of taking bribes and, as he admitted the accusation, there is no doubt that he did so. It is now generally admitted, however, that the bribes he took were no more than such as were normally taken in those days by a man in his position and that the course of Justice was in no way diverted by these bribes. His fall was no doubt caused by a plot against him rather than by any guilt which could disturb his conscience.

About 1621, and for a few years afterwards, Ben Jonson was employed by Bacon, as one of the " good pens " who were assisting him in the translation of his philosophical works into Latin, Bacon being of the opinion that Latin would be the future lingua franca of the world. Bacon was above all things anxious to preserve his reputation in the eyes of posterity. He had a very proper appreciation of the value of his own writing and took immense care to keep every document and every scrap of paper on which he had written.

How very different from Shakespeare !

Shakespeare certainly tells us several times in the sonnets that his verses will live for ever, but, as far as we know, he never made the slightest effort to ensure the preservation of any of his works.[1]

It may have been on Bacon's initiative, or at the request of Lady Pembroke, that the plays were collected and published in the First Folio, and there is an additional reason why Bacon should have undertaken this work. If he had written the plays there is no possible reason why he should not have left fair copies of the works in the hands of his literary executor with instructions to publish at some date after his death, if, for some reason, their publication was undesirable during his lifetime. But if Bacon, without being the author of the plays, had nevertheless played an important part, as I think he did by supplementing them with every variety of knowledge, Law, Latin, science and a multitude of new words, then his initiative and the difficulties with which the editors were faced become explicable, since Bacon himself would have had no fair copies of the plays. Nor would it have been possible to make use of Derby's autograph MSS.[2] without jeopardising the secret.

If the circumstances were approximately as suggested Bacon would not have had any difficulty in persuading Jonson that a literary deception was both desirable and justifiable, more particularly if this was the only way in which many of the plays could be saved for posterity. In view of the immense praise which Jonson showers on Bacon at about this time and afterwards it is not unreasonable to suspect that Bacon somewhat

---

[1] With the exception of *Venus and Adonis* and *Lucrece*.

[2] The archives of the Derby family seem to have been kept in those days in Eagle Tower, Lathom, which was burnt down in the Civil War. Probably Derby's MSS. were then destroyed.

magnified to Jonson the importance of his own contributions in the construction of the plays. Furthermore, what reason have we for believing that Jonson was so scrupulously honest that a lie could never pass his lips ? I have not the least desire to denigrate Jonson, but there is no justification for setting him up as a sort of George Washington. Jonson started life as a bricklayer—killed a man in a duel—passed some time in a debtor's prison—became a Catholic in 1598 for reasons which were certainly not wholly conscientious, and was reconverted to Protestantism, for much the same reasons, in 1610 There is nothing disgraceful about his record, but also nothing superlatively honest.

It was the custom of the age, when a poet died, for his fellow poets to write funeral odes in his honour and memory—so had Spenser been honoured in 1598, so was Jonson honoured when he died in 1637—but when Shakspere died at Stratford in 1616, no poet took the slightest notice of his death—not a mourning couplet was written—exactly as though no one had ever recognised him as a poet. It was surely going to be difficult to convince the contemporary and particularly future generations that the man who had died unhonoured and unsung was really the " Soul of the Age, the applause ! delight and Wonder of our stage." Why these sudden pæons of praise after seven years of silence ? Would people believe that this man, who had been a rich and busy farmer and landowner in Stratford for the last eighteen years of his life, was really the author of thirty-seven supreme plays, of one hundred and fifty-four sonnets and of numerous poems, two of which were dedicated to one of the great Earls ?

It was an advantage to the plan of deception that Shakspere had but seldom been seen in London during the last twenty years or more. Outside a small circle of ageing actors, few people would even remember what he looked like. As for the Stratford provincials, the Folio editors could be fairly certain that Stratford's distance from London and the prevailing illiteracy there, would prevent questions being raised regarding any statue they might choose to erect.

The first task which faced Bacon and Jonson was to find a few people who had known the actor really well, and induce them to state in writing that their friend Shakspere actually wrote the works of Shakespeare. Heminge and Condell were an obvious choice. Once their testimony had linked the First Folio and its contents to William of Stratford, Jonson could be sure that the pæons of praise and those of future generations would be delivered to the desired address.

On Bacon's sixtieth birthday, January 22nd, 1621, he gave a banquet at York House. Jonson was present and wrote an ode in his honour.

> Hail, happy genius of this ancient pile !
> How comes it all things so about thee smile ?
> The fire, the wine, the men ! and in the midst
> Thou stand'st as if some mystery thou didst ! etc.

It is not known when Jonson wrote the entries in his later *Discoveries*. These largely consisted of short notes on men whom he had encountered in his past. *No. 44* of the Temple Classics edition concerns Shakspere and I will quote it presently, for the Stratfordians lay much store by it. *No. 71* is headed Dominus Verulamis (Bacon) and I quote here a portion of it :

> . . . No man ever spoke more neatly, more presly, more weightily or suffered less emptinesse, less idleness, in what he uttered. No member of his speech but consisted of his own graces. His hearers could not cough, or look aside from him, without loss. He commanded where he spoke, and had his judges angry and pleased at his devotion. No man had their affections more in his power. The fear of every man that heard him was lest he should make an end.

This is high praise indeed from a man so learned and so critical as Ben Jonson.

No. 72 was headed Scriptorum catalogus. It starts with brief comments on the wits and orators of his time—when he comes to Bacon, however, he says :

> . . . ; Lord Egerton, the Chancellor, a grave and great orator, and best when he was provoked ; but his learned and able, though unfortunate, successor is he who hath *filled up all numbers,* and performed that in our tongue which may be compared or preferred either to *insolent Greece or haughty Rome.* In short, within his view, and about his times were all the wits born that could honour a language or help study. Now things daily fall, wits grow downward and eloquence grows backward ; so that he may be named and stand as the mark and acme of our language.

Bacon died in 1626 and these words were probably written some time in the early 1630's. It is curious to note that Jonson uses the same expression . . .

> insolent Greece or haughty Rome

in praise of Bacon as he had used about ten years before in his ode to Shakespeare in the First Folio. Thus :

> Leaue thee alone, for the comparison
> Of all that insolent Greece or haughtie Rome,
> Sent forth, or since did from their ashes come.
> > (From Jonson's Ode to Shakespeare
> > in the First Folio.)

Later, in *Discoveries,* Jonson continues his praise of Bacon.

> My conceit of his person was never increased towards him by his place or honour. But I have and do reverence him for the greatness that was only proper to himself, in that he seemed to me ever, by his work, one of the greatest of men, and most worthy of admiration, that had been in many ages. In his adversity I ever prayed that God would give him strength ; for greatness he could not want. Neither could I condole in a word or a syllable for him, as knowing no accident could do harm to virtue, but rather help to make it manifest.

As Sir George Greenwood says : " Had ever man nobler

testimony than this, which is here borne to the memory of
Bacon by one of the greatest of his contemporaries ? "

I have emphasised Jonson's opinion of Bacon to make it clear
in the first place that Bacon's influence over him must have been
very great in 1621 and the succeeding years when Jonson was
working in closest touch with him and when also the First Folio
was conceived and born. It is hard indeed to believe that in
these circumstances Jonson would have undertaken such an
important and difficult literary task without the fullest con-
sultation with Bacon and with his approval. Alternatively
if the initiative for the production of the First Folio came
from Bacon, could Jonson have refused to assist in the work ?
Secondly, I wish to emphasise the contrast between the very
high praise which Jonson gives posthumously to Bacon and the
extraordinarily unsatisfactory and rather futile remarks (*Discoveries, No. 44*) which are the only known reference made by
Jonson to Shakspeare [*sic*] subsequent to the publication of the
First Folio, viz. :

Discoveries, No. 44.

De Shakspeare Nostrati

" I remember the Players have often mentioned it as an
honour to Shakspeare that in his writing (whatsoever he penned)
he never blotted out a line. My answer hath been ' would he
had blotted out a thousand ' which they had thought a malevolent
speech. I had not told posterity this but for their ignorance
who chose that circumstance to commend their friend by
wherein he most faulted ; and to justify my own candour, for I
loved the man, and do honour his memory on this side idolatry
as much as any. He was, indeed, honest, of an open and free
nature ; had an excellent phantasy, brave notions and gentle
expressions, wherein he flowed with that facility that sometimes
it was necessary he should be stopped. ' Sufflaminandus erat ' as
Augustus said of Haterius. His wit was in his own power :

would the rule of it had been so too ! Many times he fell into those things, could not escape laughter as when he said in person of Caesar, One speaking to him, ' Caesar, thou dost me wrong.' He replied, ' Caesar did never wrong but with just cause ' ; and such like, which were ridiculous. But he redeemed his vices with his virtues. There was ever more in him to be praised than to be pardonned."

Now why did Jonson write these irritating notes and leave them for posterity—as was apparently his intention. Compare what Jonson said of Bacon in *Discoveries*, and what he says here of " Shakspeare." How utterly at variance is this paragraph with Jonson's unlimited praise of Shakespeare in 1623 ! No simple or straightforward answer can meet the case. If, how-ever, we take it as true that Jonson had been entrusted with the secret of authorship and felt in honour bound to guard it, a reasonable explanation of these notes in *Discoveries* is possible.

Let us suppose that on rereading the Preface to the First Folio Jonson suddenly realised that the prevarications about the unblotted manuscripts, etc., must inevitably destroy the whole value and force of the players' testimony. He would also know that, once their veracity was suspect, doubts must arise about Stratfordian authorship. Then, no doubt, he also remembered that he had formerly castigated the actor as Poor Poet-Ape and Sogliardo. How could future generations ever believe that Sogliardo and the " Soul of the Age " were the same man ? It was far too late for any clear circumstantial explanation, for the players' prevarications and Jonson's past sneers were unalter-able facts. I doubt whether a better method of safeguarding the secret in these difficult conditions could be found than the one adopted by Jonson.

In the first sentence he glides skilfully over the injudicious remarks in the Preface about unblotted MSS.—this was the main danger. Then Jonson says he knew " Shakspeare " personally and loved him, yet he follows this by calling him a chatterbox (sufflaminandus erat) [1] who had to be stopped. Then he damns him with faint praise and after telling a supposedly funny story about Caesar, in which he apparently laughs at the actor for misquoting the poet, he finishes by saying that Shakspeare " redeemed his vices with his virtues. There was ever more in him to be praised than to be pardonned."

After this astonishing *volte-face* concerning the man who Jonson had previously called " Soul of the Age ; The applause, Delight and wonder of our stage," no one, Stratfordian or heretic quite knows whether he is standing on his head or his heels. It does however leave a general impression, without saying so exactly, that Shakspere and Shakespeare were the same man, as if to ensure the maintenance of a deception which has survived for over three hundred years.

It is of course possible that this paragraph, *No. 44* in *Discoveries*, was written for posterity at the request of Derby with the sole purpose of strengthening the links between the First Folio and William of Stratford by fathering more securely the works of Shakespeare for all time on the actor. The deception has met with astonishing success—but then the men who supposedly devised it were of quite unusual intelligence—Derby, Bacon and Jonson.

[1] *Sufflaminandus* means " had to be stopped *talking* " — as any good Latin–English dictionary will confirm.

APPENDIX I

SHAKESPEARE'S HANDWRITING

IN 1923 a book was published by the Cambridge University Press entitled *Shakespeare's Hand in the Play of Sir Thomas More*. The authors were A. W. Pollard and others ; the others being Dr. W. W. Greg, Sir E. M. Thompson, Professor J. Dover Wilson, and Professor R. W. Chambers, so that the book has the full weight of orthodox Shakespearean scholarship behind it.

It sets out to prove, what was long believed, that Shakespeare wrote three pages of the old manuscript play *Sir Thomas More* in his own hand, composing as he wrote.

Such a discovery was obviously of outstanding interest to the literary world, but the handwriting has not yet been universally accepted with the enthusiasm which might have been expected.

Sir Thomas More was first printed in 1844 from MSS. now in the British Museum (Harl. 7368). It was Richard Simpson, a Roman Catholic theologian, who first in 1871 suggested that this portion of the play was in Shakespeare's autograph. There is no doubt that the main play was the work of several dramatists, and the date of its composition has been variously given by the best authorities as between 1590 and 1594. Calligraphically the whole manuscript has been divided into thirteen folios or pages written in a hand called S and seven pages written in five hands labelled A, B, C, D, E. Some notes were also written by the censor, who has been identified as Edmund Tilney.

The S hand which wrote the thirteen leaves is apparently Anthony Munday's. It appears that A is an authur revising someone else's or his own work ; B is found sometimes writing and sometimes making additions to his own work ; and C is a transcriber only. D is the hand which is identified as Shakespeare's, while the E hand is thought by some experts to be the hand of Thomas Dekker.[1]   It is only the D hand that we need consider here.

There are three long folios in D's hand, in all 147 lines, and I will summarise as briefly as possible the main reasons why the above Shakespearean scholars, all of highest repute, believe the D hand to be the hand of Shakespeare.

(1) Very numerous misprints are to be found in the Quartos of Shakespeare's plays for which the printers have been blamed, apparently not always justly.   Careful investigation has shown that these apparent misprints must frequently have been caused by the peculiarities or the illegibility of the author's handwriting. Professor Dover Wilson has shown, for instance, that the letters *m, n, w* as written by the author, must have been frequently indistinguishable from one another.   Any combination of these letters with one another or with *i* must have presented a very difficult problem to the printers.

Again, one can infer from misprints that *c* and *i* as written by the author, were often indistinguishable from one another.   The same may be said of *r* and *w* ; *e* and *d* ; *e* and *o*.   In this manner many of the so-called misprints would be accounted for.   Again, if the author had the habit of making an *a* like *or,* we can account for certain frequent errors which we find in the printed text.

(2) *Spelling.*   As Dover Wilson says of the spelling in Shakespeare's day—" Then a gentleman spelt as he list and only ' base mechanicals ' such as compositors spelt more or less consistently." He goes on to point out that even Gabriel Harvey, a brilliant scholar of those days, spelt in a most irregular manner.   We need not, therefore, be the least surprised at the peculiarities of Shakespeare's spelling.   In fact, by examining the misprints and spelling in the quartos, it should be possible to establish without any doubt the existence of idiosyncrasies in Shakespeare's autograph, which would make it distinguishable from that of any other writer.   Shakespeare, for instance, more frequently used

---

[1] Though recently Dr. Titherley has shown it is identical with the D hand.

y instead of *i* than other writers and he added or removed an *e* from the ends of many words according to the mood of the moment.

Supporting his thesis by a great array of examples, Dover Wilson has in fact demonstrated brilliantly not only that Shakespeare's autograph should be easily recognisable but that the D hand in the three folios of the so-called "Addition" in *Sir Thomas More* is actually the hand of Shakespeare. This cannot now be doubted and Professor Chambers has supported the whole argument of Dover Wilson on more general grounds. Indeed, the case for identifying the D hand with the hand of Shakespeare is complete, quite apart from the Shakespearean content and style, which are undeniable.

It now only remained for the experts to prove that it was the actor William Shakspere of Stratford-on-Avon who wrote the D hand. Unfortunately, the only known autographs of the Stratford actor are the six well-known signatures ; despite which Sir E. M. Thompson made a gallant, if abortive, effort to demonstrate that the same hand that wrote the six signatures also wrote the D hand.

The signatures are numbered by Thompson :

(1) The deposition ;
(2) The conveyance ;
(3) The Mortgage ;
(4) 1st page of Will ;
(5) 2nd page of Will ;
(6) 3rd page of Will.

Owing to the very limited number of letters available in the signatures, it is obvious that Thompson's task was one of great difficulty and uncertainty, to put it mildly.

Moreover No. 4 signature is so faded as to be practically unreadable. Signatures No. 2 and No. 3, written on the same or consecutive days, are not only badly written but differ very greatly from one another. The explanation, according to Thompson, is that Shakespeare thought he had to compress his signatures into the restricted space of the label on the deed. Furthermore, Thompson attributed the very poor quality of these signatures to writer's cramp. The 5th signature and the surname of the 6th are also semi-literate scrawls, not just careless writing ; and Shakespeare, said Thompson, must have been ill when he wrote them—an easy way out. There remains then only the 1st signature (the deposition) and the words " By me William " in the 6th signature, which Thompson considered as a worthy basis for comparison with Shakespeare's handwriting in hand D. The words " By me William " are excellently written. In fact, the formation of the letters and the spacing are so superior to all the rest of the signatures and to the surname which *immediately* follows, that experts now reasonably conclude that the words " By me William " were not written by Shakspere at all, but by a clerk. This, of course, would be fatal to Thompson's whole argument, which depends very largely on the well-formed letters in these three words.

So, on the above slender basis, Thompson has attempted to compare the letters formed by the D hand with the letters formed in the signatures, using mainly, but not exclusively, No. 1 signature and the unacceptable words " By me William."

It is remarkable that in the D hand, each letter of the alphabet is formed in several different ways, and Thompson has given us an extremely interesting page showing nearly every variation of every letter in the D hand side by side with the very sparse letters of the signatures.

The result is wholly unconvincing. It has not, in fact, convinced even the great majority of orthodox Shakespearean scholars, eager as they would naturally be to accept such a satisfactory conclusion. So the D hand cannot be identified with that of Shakspere of Stratford by any stretch of imagination.

This is the present position, or was, till the recent appearance of Dr. A. W. Titherley's work, *Shakespeare's Identity*, which, unless rebutted, completely revolutionises the whole situation. It is not possible to enter deeply into Dr. Titherley's elaborate calligraphic analysis which confirms Professor Dover Wilson's proof that the D hand in *Sir Thomas More* is the hand of Shakespeare beyond the least doubt.

When Professors Wilson, Pollard and the others wrote their book in 1923, a search was made among autographs of all known dramatists of Shakespeare's day to find out whether any of them wrote in a hand resembling the D hand, but without success. No one, of course, in 1922 thought of examining the autographs of the 6th Earl of Derby. Now, Dr. Titherley not only finds, by meticulously careful comparison, that the D hand and Derby's hand reproduce each other down to the last detail, including handwriting idiosyncrasies of most varied kinds, but has shown that the rather numerous and sometimes unusual variations used by Derby for each letter of the alphabet are the actual variations used by D. More than this, he has proved that both Derby and D show similar frequencies in favoured letter varieties, and the same average letter dimensions and spacing. In fact, the more critically Dr. Titherley's exposition is studied and the more thoroughly individual letter variations and flourishes of each hand are compared, the more certain does it become that the writer of the D hand and the 6th Earl of Derby were one and the same man. But Dover Wilson (*et al*) have already proved conclusively that the writer of the D hand is Shakespeare himself. . . .

APPENDIX II

SUMMARY OF EVIDENCE

FOR the convenience of readers I have here summarised the evidence proving that Shakespeare was the 6th Earl of Derby, the only man who *completely* meets my specification, (p. 13) whatever assistance he may have obtained from the "magic circle."

1. A favourite resort of William Stanley, both before and after he became Earl, seems to have been Meriden Manor, one of the Derby family seats, near to which Holinshed lived and died. It is in the old Forest of Arden in North Warwickshire. This region rather than that around Stratford-on-Avon contains the names of numerous places mentioned in the plays—e.g., Falstaff's March.

2. William Stanley is reported by Seacome, his first historian, to have been an extremely industrious boy, thirsting for knowledge of every kind.

3. At eleven years old he matriculated at St. John's College, Oxford, a college noted in those days for its interest in drama.

4. After leaving Oxford, Stanley completed his studies (làw, etc.) at Gray's Inn. There he would have met Bacon, and later Southampton, and also many other men of highest culture.

5. When twenty-one he went abroad with his tutor, Richard Lloyd. He stayed in Paris from July to October 1582 at the Court of Henri III. Whilst there, all the incidents now known (Lambin) to underlie *Measure for Measure* took place before his eyes.

6. Stanley alone of all possible candidates could have been at Nerac at the Court of Henri of Navarre in 1583 and so have learnt first-hand of the various events there on which *Love's Labour's Lost* is based. The play teems with intimate recollections of life at this Court and the principal characters are easily recognised French historical personages who were there at that time.

7. Richard Lloyd, Stanley's pedantic tutor, who accompanied

him, was the actual author of the pageant *The Nine Worthies*, which was parodied by Shakespeare in *Love's Labour's Lost*. Lloyd himself was no doubt caricatured as Holofernes.

8. Stanley spent about five years abroad and echoes of his travels repeatedly appear in the plays—for example, *All's Well*, *Two Gentlemen of Verona*, *Merchant of Venice*, *The Taming of the Shrew*, etc., in all of which topographical familiarity is revealed. He also is recorded to have travelled extensively in E. Mediterranean (*Othello* and *Pericles*) and to Egypt (*Antony and Cleopatra*). He also visited Constantinople and Russia, and perhaps Germany, Denmark and the Netherlands, where he may have seen war in 1586 with Leicester's expedition. Places abroad not visited by Stanley rarely appear in the plays.

9. He returned to England in 1587 and was present when the Leicester players came up directly from Stratford to Lathom. Shakspere probably came up with these players, because some of Leicester's men next year joined Lord Strange's company (Stanley's brother) and in Strange's company (later The Lord Chamberlain's) Shakspere spent all his acting life. This company had a virtual monopoly of the Shakespeare plays. Thus Stanley could have met Shakspere at Lathom and then or later appointed him as his agent.

10. In 1591 Edmund Spenser dedicated *The Tears of the Muses* to Alice, wife of Ferdinando (Stanley's brother and later 5th Earl of Derby). In this poem Spenser praises " Our pleasant Willy " as a brilliant poet and comedy writer. The word " Our " thus reasonably indicates a member of the Derby family and there is no one else called " Willy " who can possibly fit all the words and circumstances but William Stanley.

11. Spenser in 1594, in his poem *Colin Clouts come Home again* mourns in twelve lines the death of Stanley's brother (Ferdinando) and sympathises with the sorrow of Ferdinando's wife, Alice. In the next four lines he praises Ætion (eagle) as a great poet. Ætion can only be Stanley, now the head of the House of Derby.

Both the allusions (Willy and Ætion) are admitted by competent critics to be in praise of Shakespeare.

12. In 1591, William Stanley fell in love with Elizabeth de Vere, daughter of the Earl of Oxford. According to both Chambers and Titherley, it was during the festivities at Elvetham in 1591, given by the Earl of Hertford in honour of the Queen, that the romance started ; Elizabeth de Vere being a maid of honour to the Queen. Many incidents at this fête are reflected in *Midsummer Night's Dream*, which was written specially (Chambers and Titherley) to be played on the night of Derby's marriage before the Queen and the Court at Greenwich.

Surely it must have been Derby who there recalled these memories of his private life in a play written as a wedding gift to his bride.

13. Derby's wedding was postponed from the middle of 1594 till January 26th, 1595. There is evidence that the Queen, soon after Stanley became the 6th Earl of Derby, considered making him her Consort. As Derby was tolerant of Catholics, this would have been a good act of statesmanship, and in any case Derby was a legal pretender to the throne. She rejected him, as she had rejected so many others, and gave the excuse that he had demeaned himself by amateur acting—or so it seems from Davies' epigram to Shakespeare (p. 94).

14. It was during this time of uncertainty and unhappiness in 1594, when Derby thought he might be compelled to relinquish Elizabeth de Vere and marry the Queen, that certain farewell sonnets were written by him to Elizabeth (Titherley, who also thus explains the dirge in *Phœnix and the Turtle*).

15. Ever since 1488 the Derby family had been keen patrons of drama and frequently attended the Chester Midsummer and Whitsun plays, various incidents of which are reflected in Shakespeare's plays (*Midsummer Night's Dream* and *Hamlet*). Chester was Derby's favourite town on the Welsh border, to which he retired and where he died.

16. *Midsummer Night's Dream* has been proved by Lefranc to reflect the crude efforts of the Chester artisans patronised by the Stanleys and represented by Bottom, Flute, etc. In this play, as both Chambers and Titherley agreed, Theseus truly impersonates Derby and Hyppolita his bride Elizabeth de Vere. Moreover, Oberon's speech symbolises the Queen's rejection of Derby's suit and the descent of Cupid's love-shaft on the " little western flower," Elizabeth de Vere.

17. In 1599 Derby withdrew to a cottage at Hedingham with his wife to write plays ; for he was then reported by Fenner, a Jesuit agent, as " interested only in penning comedies for the common players."

18. In 1593, when Stanley was, as yet, only the second son of an Earl, *Venus and Adonis* was published, with a respectful dedication to the Earl of Southampton. This poem the author called " the first heir of my invention," having evidently been written by Stanley during his travels in Greece in 1585 (Titherley). *Lucrece,* published in 1594, after Derby became Earl, was also dedicated to Southampton, but in familiar terms such as one Earl might address to another.

19. Both *Venus* and *Lucrece* were " seen through the press " by the author—thereafter Shakespeare took no personal interest in the publication of any of his works. The reason offered is that as a possible Consort to the Queen and a potential successor, Derby had now to be specially careful to conceal the authorship, more particularly of such a play as *Richard II,* which was considered traitorous by Queen Elizabeth and was actually used by Essex to stir up rebellion against her.

20. In the historical plays there are numerous instances where the ancestors of both Derby and Oxford are given more important rôles than is justified by the history sources (mainly Holinshed and Hall).

21. Derby being Oxford's son-in-law, it is not surprising to find in some plays—e.g., *Hamlet* and *Othello,* and others—

reflections of incidents in Oxford's life, as well as in Derby's.

22. *The Merry Wives of Windsor* contains irrelevant allusions to the Garter ceremony and to a Star Chamber case simulating that of Proctor *versus* Derby. Derby had just received the honour of K.G. and Stephen Proctor in the Star Chamber was actually accusing Derby's agent of exactly the same offences as those of which Shallow accuses Falstaff in the play. Proctor's name was even in the first edition of this play but not in later editions, i.e., when the action was settled.

23. For fourteen years, from 1594–1608, Derby was in serious financial difficulties owing to a lawsuit contesting his estates and title as King of the Isle of Man : in the latter part of this troubled period the plays took on a more bitter quality (*Hamlet,* etc.).

24. The Great Tragedies were composed at a time when Derby was desperately unhappy owing to domestic as well as these financial troubles. He not only had grave suspicions concerning the fidelity of his wife, but anxieties from the great lawsuit which dragged on endlessly, eating up his fortune. He may also have felt keen disappointment at not succeeding to the throne in 1603.

25. *Cymbeline, Winter's Tale* and *The Tempest* were written on the theme of reconciliation after the lawsuit had been settled and Derby had been confirmed by James I once more as King of Man.

26. *The Tempest,* involving John Dee's benevolent system of magic, could only have been written by a man of sufficient rank to disregard James's violent obsession against magic. Derby was in constant touch with Dee both in Lancashire and London.

27. A very large number of truly Shakespearean alterations and improvements were made in several plays, apparently and, in the case of *Richard III,* certainly after the death of Shakspere and Oxford. Of all possible candidates, only Bacon and Derby were alive 1620–23, and Bacon is excluded for reasons given (page 18).

28. Derby retired and lived quietly, mainly at Chester, about

the time the First Folio was published 1623. There is no reason why he should not have continued to revise his plays up to that date, as we know Shakespeare did constantly. When revising *Richard III* he must have utilised the 1622 Quarto. See (p. 111).

29. The frequent contemporary use of the hyphenated name Shake-speare clearly signifies that it was not a surname but a *nom de plume*. It was well known at the time that various noblemen were writing poetry, which it was *infra dig.* for them to publish under their own names. But Derby had even more serious reasons for maintaining secrecy (page 127).

30. The prominence which Shakespeare gives to Welsh people and to Welsh affairs and to Wales itself, just across the border from Chester, is another pointer to Derby as author. Northern dialect and numerous dialectical words peculiar to Lancashire are used in the plays, as well as Northern *s*-plurals, employed with much greater frequency by Shakespeare than by any other dramatist (Titherley). Shakespeare certainly knew Lancashire and Cheshire very intimately.

31. Derby's great erudition, unusual travel experiences and whole life and character are entirely congruous to his identity with Shakespeare. He was a scholar, a linguist and a musical composer with a lawyer's training and a soldier's experience of war and almost a sailor's knowledge of the sea. He had well-stocked libraries and ample leisure and also every opportunity to share the knowledge of the most deeply learned men of France, Italy and England. Bacon and John Dee were his friends and he was intimately acquainted with that astonishing clique of aristocratic scholars and poets who surrounded Queen Elizabeth.

32. Shakespeare's vocabulary of fifteen to twenty thousand words, including a vast number of new words derived from Latin and French, proves that the author was a scholar and a linguist.

33. It is obvious from the plays that Shakespeare was a consummate statesman like all the Stanleys.

34. The 4th Earl of Derby's steward, William Ffarrington,

was without doubt caricatured as Malvolio (Lefranc, Thaler and Titherley).

35. In the very personal Sonnet 136 the poet states explicitly that his name is Will, as Derby always signed himself; never William, which was used only in the pen-name (Titherley).

36. John Donne's sonnet to E. of D., by its contents, reasonably shows that he was addressing Shakespeare in person. At that time (1618) there was no other poet-Earl, E. of D. possible, but Derby.

37. Certain poems, some signed W. S. (earliest 1577), have been critically examined by Titherley and proved to be early experiments of William Stanley. These poems, at first immature, all display true Shakespearean characteristics with developing power and overflowing rhythm. No one else with initials W. S. could possibly have written them but William Stanley. One of the poems of this group exists in manuscript, viz., The " Mistress " poem of the *Passionate Pilgrim* (long accepted as Shakespearean) and is actually in Stanley's autograph. Another, the " Dowland " sonnet, written about 1591 (published 1598), admits that he, Shakespeare, is a Knight (as Stanley seems to have been in 1591). The date 1598 excludes Bacon, who was knighted in 1603.

38. There is nothing in the life or character of Derby—as there is in the lives of all other candidates, Oxford, Rutland, Bacon and Shakspere—which is incongruous to Derby as Shakespeare. All new discoveries have fitted into this picture like pieces into a jigsaw puzzle.

39. Lastly and decisively, the " D " handwriting in the MSS. play *Sir Thomas More,* which Dover Wilson and others have proved to be the genuine writing of Shakespeare, has now been proved by Titherley to be the hand of William Stanley by rigorous calligraphic analysis (see Appendix I).

Note. The references (Titherley) are to Dr. A. W. Titherley's work, *Shakespeare's Identity.*

BIBLIOGRAPHY

The following are among the books consulted :

FOR THE ORTHODOX CASE

Shakespeare. Third Variorum. 1821. By Edmund Malone.
Outlines. 6th Edition. 1886. By J. O. Halliwell-Phillipps.
Shakespeare. 2 vols. By E. K. Chambers.
Life of Shakespeare. 1915. By Sidney Lee.
Shakespeare : *Encyclopædia Britannica.* By E. K. Chambers.
Shakespeare's Hand in " Sir Thomas More." 1923. By Pollard and others.
The Bacon-Shakespeare Question. 1888. By C. Stopes.
A Chapter in the Early Life of Shakespeare. 1927. By Arthur Gray.
The Amazing Monument. 1939. By Ivor Brown.
Introducing Shakespeare. By G. B. Harrison.
England of Elizabeth. By A. L. Rouse.
The Man Shakespeare. 1909. By Frank Harris.
Life of the Earl of Southampton. By C. Stopes.
The Essential Shakespeare. By J. Dover Wilson.

AGAINST THE ORTHODOX CASE

Shakespeare Identified. 1920. By J. T. Looney.
Alias William Shakespeare. 1947. By Claud W. Sykes.
Shakespeare's Vital Secret. 1937. By J. Macdonald Lucas.
Sous le Masque de William Shakespeare. 1919. By Abel Lefranc.
New Views for Old. 1930. By Roderick Eagle.
Bacon is Shakespeare. 1910. By Edwin Durning-Laurence.
The Shakespeare Problem Restated. 1908. By George Greenwood.
Seven Shakespeares. 1931. By Gilbert Slater.
Shakespeare's Sonnets and Edward de Vere. 1930. By Canon Rendall.
The Seventeenth Earl of Oxford. 1928. By B. M. Ward.
Who was Shakespeare ? 1955. By H. Amphlett.

INDEX

Note.—The author having adopted the device of spelling "Shakespeare" when referring to the author ("whoever he may be") of the plays and poems, and "Shakspere" when referring to the actor William, of Stratford, entries appear under those respective headings. Titles of plays and poems are in italics. The letter "f" indicates that the reference is in a footnote.